KNOWING

ALSO BY TOURÉ ROBERTS

Purpose Awakening: Discover the Epic Idea That Motivated Your Birth

Wholeness: Winning in Life from the Inside Out

Balance: Positioning Yourself to Do All Things Well

KNOWING

THE JOURNEY TO
CERTAINTY IN AN
UNCERTAIN WORLD

TOURÉ ROBERTS

ZONDERVAN
BOOKS

ZONDERVAN BOOKS

Knowing

Published by Zondervan, 3950 Sparks Drive SE, Suite 101, Grand Rapids, MI 49546, USA. Zondervan is a registered trademark of The Zondervan Corporation, L.L.C., a wholly owned subsidiary of HarperCollins Christian Publishing, Inc.

Requests for information should be addressed to customercare@harpercollins.com.

Zondervan titles may be purchased in bulk for educational, business, fundraising, or sales promotional use. For information, please email SpecialMarkets@Zondervan.com.

ISBN 978-0-310-37115-1 (audio)

Library of Congress Cataloging-in-Publication Data

Names: Roberts, Touré author
Title: Knowing : the journey to certainty in an uncertain world / Touré Roberts.
Description: Grand Rapids, MI, USA : Zondervan Books, [2026] | Includes biographical information.
Identifiers: LCCN 2025054237 (print) | LCCN 2025054238 (ebook) | ISBN 9780310371120 hardcover | ISBN 9780310371144 ebook
Subjects: LCSH: Knowledge, Theory of (Religion) | Certainty | Christian life
Classification: LCC BT40 .R555 2026 (print) | LCC BT40 (ebook)
LC record available at https://lccn.loc.gov/2025054237
LC ebook record available at https://lccn.loc.gov/2025054238

HarperCollins Publishers, Macken House, 39/40 Mayor Street Upper, Dublin 1, D01 C9W8, Ireland (https://www.harpercollins.com)

Cover design: Mila Book Cover Designer
Cover illustrations: Shutterstock / iStock / Alamy
Interior design: Sara Colley

Printed in the United States of America

26 27 28 29 30 LBC 6 5 4 3 2

I dedicate this book to the greatest inspirations to me on the planet: my children, Ren, Teya, Isaiah, Malachi, Makenzie, Ella, and my son-in-love Tyler!

You mean the world to me, and if you were the only people ever to read this book, it was worth all it cost me to write it.

I love you.

CONTENTS

FOREWORD

BY ELLA ROBERTS (AGE 9)

A NOTE FROM THE AUTHOR

And a little child shall lead them.

—Isaiah 11:6

OKAY, I'VE GOT A CONFESSION TO MAKE.

The next few words you will read were not written by Ella, though you'll hear from her in just a moment.

This is her dad.

And I already know what you might be thinking: Why would a nine-year-old be the one chosen to write the foreword to a book about something as deep and divine as Knowing?

After all, I could've asked a theologian.

A psychologist.

A scholar.

Some of the greatest spiritual and intellectual minds in the world are within reach for me. I have access to the best. And any one of them would've made perfect sense.

But I didn't choose them. I chose a child—intentionally.

Because Knowing doesn't always come with age.

Sometimes it comes with proximity—proximity to wonder, to purity, to the unfiltered voice of God.

Children are born close to that voice.

They carry a kind of clarity the world hasn't yet talked them out of.

They don't overthink it.

They don't question it.

They just know.

And if Knowing truly is our first sense—as I propose in these pages—then a child is often still aware of what many of us spend our lives trying to rediscover.

Ella didn't write from experience. She wrote from essence.

She didn't write as someone who has walked a hundred miles. She wrote as someone who more clearly remembers where we all began.

So before you meet her words, I invite you to pause. To open not just your eyes but your heart. Because what comes next is not childish, it's childlike. And in that there is power.

Now with reverence and expectation, I give you Ella.

ELLA'S FOREWORD

When my dad said he was writing a book, I asked him, "Can I write the foreword?" I'm not really sure why I said it. I just felt it in my heart. I didn't know what the book was going to be about, but something inside me told me I should be part of it.

And the funny thing is, he said yes.

At first, it probably seemed like a strange question. I mean, I'm only nine. But sometimes kids just know things. We don't always have the perfect words, but we still feel the truth. My dad says that grown-ups can forget that kind of Knowing. But kids still have it. Maybe because our hearts are still open.

Sometimes I feel things really strongly.

Like, I'll say something, and my parents will look at each other kind of surprised and say, "How did you know that?"

And I'll just say, "I don't know—I just did."

That kind of thing happens a lot. Sometimes I finish people's sentences, even if they didn't say anything yet. Or I'll say exactly what someone else was thinking before they even open their mouth. One time, we were traveling out of the country, and our tour guide was trying really hard to explain something. She couldn't quite find the right word. And even though she hadn't told me much, I gave her the word she was looking for—and it was exactly right. She was so surprised. But to me it just felt normal.

That's what this book is about. Not learning something new but remembering something that's already inside you. A kind of Knowing that comes from deep inside, not from your brain but from your heart.

When my dad and I talked, we started wondering about what happens when people stop trusting that feeling. That's when I said, "If you doubt it, it won't work."

And I really meant it. If you stop believing in that quiet voice inside, it starts to fade. But if you trust it—even if it doesn't make total sense—it gets stronger. It starts helping you.

I also said, "It's kind of like the wind. You can't see it, but you feel it. And sometimes you just know something in your heart, not because someone told you but because it's just there."

And maybe that's what this book is for: to help you feel that again, to help you remember how to trust it.

So before you start reading, I just want to ask, Can you be open? Can you read this like a kid would, without trying to figure everything out?

Because sometimes your heart understands before your head does.

And sometimes the best way to know something is to feel it.

And remember, if you doubt it, it won't work.

Love,
Ella

INTRODUCING KNOWING

I DON'T KNOW IF THERE HAS EVER BEEN A TIME IN OUR world when uncertainty has been as unrelenting as it is today.

It's everywhere. In everything. It grips us all.

Uncertainty doesn't show deference to the rich over the poor, the conservative over the progressive, or the educated over the illiterate. The religious doesn't get a pass, nor does the agnostic gain an advantage. It doesn't matter who you are, if you live in this world, you are affected by it.

Uncertainty is indifferent to race, tribe, or class. And there is no escaping it.

Even if you packed your bags and fled to some distant land of your dreams, uncertainty would meet you there—waiting, patient, relentless.

It's as if a perfectly mixed cocktail of instability, volatility, and ambiguity has been served for us all to drink—a brew that not even the most prudent, privileged, or prepared can avoid.

You can be wise and still feel lost. You can be prayerful and still feel pressure. You can be surrounded by people and still feel alone.

Uncertainty isn't just about what's happening around us, it's also about what starts happening within us.

Uncertainty has a way of creeping past the headlines and into our homes. Into our hearts. Into our thoughts at night when the world is quiet but our minds are loud.

And lately it's been showing up everywhere.

The economy is unstable. Prices are rising. Families are stretched thin, struggling to afford even basic necessities. Global markets are fragile. Debt is mounting, personally and nationally. The financial security we once relied on feels more like a memory.

Political division runs deep. Trust in leadership and systems is eroding. Institutions that were meant to protect democracy now feel paper thin under pressure. Facts feel flexible. Lies wear suits. And many have stopped believing that truth even exists anymore.

Fear, once a whisper, now shouts in the minds of many. Domestic terrorism and mass shootings haunt public spaces. The once simple act of gathering—at concerts, malls, or even church—now carries a quiet undercurrent of caution.

And then there's the climate. Floods, fires, hurricanes, record-breaking heat waves. The earth groans, and so do we. "Normal" is no longer a stable reference point. Seasons feel unfamiliar. Even time seems to be moving differently.

Wars rage. Tensions rise. Nations shake. And many are quietly asking, What in the world is happening? And where can I find something solid to stand on?

I realize this probably isn't the uplifting message you'd expect at the beginning of a book that promises to change your life. But before we get to the promise, we have to acknowledge the pain. We have to tell the truth.

I see it. I feel it. I live in this world too. But I want you to know something: I'm not gripped by it like I used to be. The headlines still swirl. The chaos is still real. But my internal world is different.

I've discovered something that changed my life. Something deeper than information. Something stronger than positivity. Something that has anchored me in a drifting world.

It didn't come overnight. It came through pain. Through transformation. Through unlearning. Through surrender. Through learning to be still when everything in me wanted to run.

It came through a sacred process. And it's what this book is about.

It's called Knowing.

Knowing is hard to explain in one sentence—because it's not just one thing. It's part awareness, part revelation. Part instinct, part clarity. It's the peace that keeps you steady in a storm and the courage that leads you to speak when the room is silent.

Knowing is both a foundation and a compass. It is the first sense, the divine imprint in your spirit that helps you perceive what your eyes can't yet see. It's not just what you think, it's what you perceive. It's not just what you hear, it's what you discern.

It's how you recognize truth when deception is dressed up in beauty. It's how you build a life that can't be shaken by external storms. It's how you move forward when the path hasn't yet been paved.

Knowing is how you make decisions that don't make sense on paper but make perfect sense in the context of purpose. And when activated, it becomes a force—one that unlocks peace, power, confidence, and alignment.

I didn't always recognize it. It took years. It took missteps. It took losses and recoveries. But when I did, I realized Knowing had been guiding me all along.

It helped me walk away from what looked perfect on paper. It protected me from missteps I would've paid for. It whispered wisdom when logic failed. It gave me the courage to pivot, the strength to endure, and the confidence to build.

It helped me trust again when trust had been broken. It helped me stay still when everything in me wanted to act out of fear. It helped me see who I really was, beneath the labels, beneath the pain, beneath the striving.

Everything I am today, everything I've built, everything I will become is a result of listening to what I Know.

And the same is true for you.

This book is your invitation to rediscover the voice beneath the noise, the truth beneath the trauma, and the clarity beneath the chaos.

If you've been anxious about the future, Knowing will ground you. If you've felt stuck or stagnant, Knowing will give you the courage to move. If you've lost yourself in disappointment or delay, Knowing will bring you home again.

And if life has caused you to forget who you are, Knowing will help you remember.

Throughout these pages you'll encounter stories, insights, tools, and truths that will enable you to do the following:

- Recognize your inner Knowing
- Unlearn what trauma taught you
- Speak and live with spiritual alignment
- Wait when it's unclear
- Trust when it hurts
- Walk in certainty, even when the world doesn't make sense

You'll learn that trauma doesn't just wound you, it can rewire you. But Knowing is how you heal. Knowing is how you recover the truth. Knowing is how you rebuild from the inside out.

This is more than a book. It's a return. A reintroduction. A divine invitation.

It's a call to reawaken your spiritual instincts. To rebuild the temple of your mind. To rediscover your divine design. And to live boldly in a world that desperately needs light.

So now, beloved, let us Know. And let us grow.

ONE

BE STILL AND KNOW

IF COCOONS COULD TALK

Before we begin what I believe will be a powerful, enlightening, and transformational journey, one that I trust will guide you to a place of deep confidence and assurance no matter what's happening around you, I feel it would be disingenuous not to share the space I found myself in just days before sitting down to write this book.

I wish I could tell you I felt on top of the world, the way I did when I first mapped out the outline for this guide—full of clarity, fired up by a mission, and certain of the power this message holds. I wish I could tell you that the transformational tools and spiritual perspectives you'll encounter in these pages were already firmly in my grasp, that I was standing squarely in the grounded, unwavering place that Knowing leads us to.

But the truth is, I wasn't. Not even close.

In those early moments before I began writing, I felt weak. Uncertain. Unsure about my life and where things were headed in our world. Not exactly the creative space you dream of when setting out to write a book meant to uplift and empower others.

I felt vulnerable. Exposed. And if I'm being fully honest, deep down, I was doubting myself.

The consortium of uncertainty swirling in my own life had begun to weigh heavily on me. And I could feel my confidence slipping, not dramatically, not loudly, but steadily. Like air quietly seeping from a balloon. No rupture, no warning. Just a slow, steady unraveling of what once gave me lift.

During better times I had coined the phrase *radical optimism*. It had become my mantra. It accurately described my baseline temperament, and I often used it to inspire others to be hopeful, steadfast, and positive regardless of current circumstances. But on this day radical optimism had packed its bags, left no forwarding address, and wasn't answering texts. I sat there unsure, unmotivated, and, frankly, unbothered by the idea of staying under the covers indefinitely. The confidence I usually carried like a torch had fizzled into the sad flicker of a flashlight from the junk drawer, weak, sputtering, and mostly only lighting my doubts. My once vibrant mantra started to feel like an inside joke God was telling, only I wasn't in on the punchline. I felt like the biggest impostor in the world. How could I call myself a teacher on the subject when I felt as though I needed to re-enroll in the basics myself? How could I guide anyone else into Knowing when I barely recognized the path?

As I stepped back and began to reflect on what I was walking through, the irony became painfully clear: To guide others toward a deeper sense of Knowing, I first had to survive my own unraveling. I couldn't just rely on the tools that had carried me this far. They weren't enough. I had to dig deeper, reach higher, and discover new tools I didn't even know I had. Tools forged not in clarity but in chaos. Not in certainty but in the shaking.

And that brings me to something essential we must all understand about Knowing: It isn't a static state. It evolves. It stretches. It deepens. Knowing is not a single mountaintop. It's a layered experience, revealed level by level as we grow. And between each level lies a space that feels like emptiness, like ignorance. Later in this book, we'll explore how ignorance isn't the enemy of Knowing but often the catalyst to it.

Between those successive levels of clarity, we pass through a kind of in-between space. A fog. A wilderness. A purgatory, even. It can feel disorienting, even painful. But if we stay with it—if we trust the process—we emerge changed. We emerge clearer, stronger, and more grounded in who we are and what we know.

There are some foundational things you must know from the outset—truths that create the framework for your growth and establish the environment where deeper levels of Knowing can take root. It's on this framework that the incomparable experience of Knowing is built. I've come to realize that in order to be transported from one level of Knowing to the next, we often have to be grounded again in the basics. Why? Because the path of evolution in Knowing is not a straight line, it's a cocoon. This cocoon is a holding place between what was and what will be. A space designed by God for shedding the old and shaping the new. How you endure the cocoon determines how you emerge. It holds transformation, yes, but also confusion, isolation, and silence. There are certain things the cocoon won't explain. It won't give you a road map. You just have to Know, on a deeper level, what's true when everything familiar seems to disappear.

Let's take a moment to better understand the cocoon.

At times, the cocoon forms when uncertainty takes over. When your personal world or the world around you feels unstable, your optimism fades, and the solid ground of your Knowing begins to give way. It doesn't feel like part of a clearly marked process. It feels like something to survive. Uncertainty wraps around you like a weighted blanket. Not comforting but heavy, settling over your thoughts and making it harder to move forward. It clouds your vision, shakes your confidence, and makes even the most familiar truths feel distant. You begin to question everything, even yourself.

And yet, even in that disorienting stillness, something deeper may be taking place. The cocoon, however it begins, can become a sacred space of transformation. Whether it was triggered by chaos or divinely woven for your growth, the cocoon holds more than confusion. Is it awkward? Yes. Uncomfortable? Without question. But it can also be purposeful. A hidden passage that prepares you, reworks you, and ultimately readies you to fly.

Knowing how to navigate that space, whether it came upon you suddenly or formed itself around you gradually over time, is essential. The darkness may feel the same, dense, silent, and displacing. But what you hold on to in that space will shape who you become.

If cocoons could talk, they'd remind you that disorientation doesn't mean you're lost, it might mean that you're being remade.

Here are five truths you must know when you find yourself in the cocoon.

FIVE THINGS YOU MUST KNOW IN THE COCOON OF UNCERTAINTY

1. GOD KNOWS EXACTLY WHERE YOU ARE

> "But he knows where I am going.
> And when he tests me, I will come out as pure as gold."
>
> —*Job 23:10 NLT*

When you're in the cocoon of uncertainty, one of the most important things you must remember is this: Even when you feel lost, you are never invisible. God knows exactly where you are, physically, emotionally, spiritually. You may feel off course. You may feel forgotten. But you're not. You're seen, you're known, and you're held by the one who has never lost track of you.

I don't think there's a better witness to this truth than a man named Job. You may be familiar with him. He had what we might lightly call a rough season. In a short span of time, Job lost everything—his wealth, his health, his family, his reputation. The life he once knew disintegrated before his eyes. If anyone knew the weight of uncertainty and pain, it was him.

And yet, somewhere in the middle of that unraveling, Job tapped into a deeper truth. A Knowing that came not from his circumstances but from something more rooted. He said, "But he knows where I am going."

Job didn't say that he himself knew where he was going. In fact, he likely had no idea what tomorrow would bring. But he held on to this: God knew.

God knew his location. God knew his heart. God knew the outcome. And that was enough to steady him in the dark.

When Job wrote those words, he wasn't speaking from a mountaintop, he was buried deep in the valley. And still he was able to say, in faith, "When he tests me, I will come out as pure as gold."

That's not denial. That's not blind optimism. That's Knowing.

Job came to understand that what he was walking through wasn't meaningless. It was refining. It was forming. It was divinely orchestrated. What he was sitting in felt like death, but it was actually transformation. He was in a cocoon. Not abandoned, but being shaped. Not discarded, but being developed.

And, in time, he would emerge not just intact but renewed.

If God knew exactly where Job was, he knows exactly where you are too.

Takeaway

God doesn't lose people. Not in pain. Not in the metamorphosis process. Not even in the dark.

For Reflection

- What would change in you today if you truly believed that God knows exactly where you are, even if you don't?

2. WHEN YOU CAN'T SEE GOD'S HAND, YOU CAN TRUST HIS HEART

"Though he slay me, yet will I trust in him."

—Job 13:15 KJV

There are moments on the journey—especially when you're deep in the cocoon—when you can't see what God is doing. His hand feels hidden. His movement isn't obvious. And in those moments doubt starts whispering: *Has God left me? Does he care about me and what I am facing?*

This is where trust stops being a concept and becomes a choice.

Job, once again, becomes our guide here. After all he had been through—the loss, the isolation, the unanswered questions—he made a statement that almost feels irrational: "Though he slay me, yet will I trust in him." Pause on that for a moment. Job was saying this: *Even if God's plan ends in my death, I will still trust him*. Why? Because he trusted not just God's actions but God's character. He believed in God's integrity, God's love, and God's faithfulness even when none of it made sense.

Job's circumstances didn't point to goodness. They pointed to tragedy. But somewhere deep in his spirit he knew: *God's heart for me is still good. Even if the outcome doesn't look like what I hoped, even if I never get the answers I want, even if I don't survive this season—I trust him*. That's the kind of Knowing that anchors you when life is unraveling. It's not passive. It's not naive. It's fierce, defiant trust in the middle of uncertainty. It's saying, *Even if I can't trace his hand, I will not question his heart*.

Because the heart of God is for me. Always.
Even when it doesn't feel that way.
Even when it hurts.
Even when it's silent.

Takeaway

Faith is not always about understanding God's plan. Sometimes it's simply trusting God's nature.

For Reflection

- When have you seen God's heart redeem a situation you didn't understand in the moment?
- If you believed God's heart was always for you, how would that shift the way you walk through this season?

3. YOU ARE SAFE IN THE COCOON

> "For I know the plans I have for you," declares the LORD, "plans to prosper you and not to harm you, plans to give you hope and a future."
>
> —*Jeremiah 29:11 NIV*

This verse has comforted generations. It's printed on mugs, journals, and graduation cards, and for good reason. It speaks of hope, future, and divine intention. But what many people don't realize is *when* this promise was spoken.

God gave these words to his people as they were about to enter captivity, not freedom. He was essentially saying, "You're about to go through something hard. It's going to last a long time. But I know what I'm doing."

In other words: "You're safe. Even in this."

Their captivity—seventy long years of exile—was their cocoon.

It wasn't ideal. It wasn't glamorous. But it was part of a larger plan. It was a space of containment and transformation. And while it was difficult, it was not destructive.

God's people weren't being abandoned. They were being preserved.

This is one of the most profound things we can know in our own cocoon seasons: Even if it feels like everything is falling apart, you are not in danger, you are in process.

The cocoon may feel restrictive. It may feel dark. It may feel isolating. But it is also a place of protection and provision. A prepared place, designed by a God who knows what's on the other side.

You are safe in the cocoon, not because the conditions are comfortable but because the one who placed you there is trustworthy.

He is not punishing you. He is preparing you.

He is not hiding from you. He is holding you.

And even when you don't feel safe, you are secure in his hands.

Takeaway

The cocoon may not be comfortable, but it *is* covered. You are held, even here.

For Reflection

- What if the place you are resenting right now is the very place God is using to protect and prepare you?

4. COCOONS ARE TEMPORARY

> For our light and momentary affliction is producing for us an eternal weight of glory far beyond comparison.
>
> —*2 Corinthians 4:17 BSB*

Here's something else you need to know about the cocoon: It won't last forever. Even if it feels endless. Even if the days are long and the nights stretch out like years. Even if you've lost track of time and momentum and you can't remember what it feels like to move forward. This cocoon is temporary. This is a passage, not a prison.

Scripture tells us that "our light and momentary troubles are achieving for us an eternal glory that far outweighs them all" (NIV). Now, let's be honest. When you're in the thick of your struggle, *light* and *momentary* are the last words you'd use to describe it.

It's painful.

It's heavy.

It feels never-ending.

But what Scripture is doing here is giving us a heavenly lens, a long view. It's not minimizing suffering. It's reminding us that what feels unbearable now will one day be seen as necessary. What feels like a crushing delay now will one day be recognized as the pressure that gave birth to something priceless in you.

From the outside, the cocoon looks dormant. Lifeless, even. But on the inside? Metamorphosis. That's what your process is doing: transforming you in ways you can't yet see. But make no mistake—it's moving you forward.

As you endure your cocoon season, remember: You're not stuck, you're being carried. This moment isn't final. It's formative. This discomfort isn't forever. It's divine.

It's okay to groan. It's okay to grieve. But don't give up. The work happening in you is holy, and it has an end date.

Takeaway

This isn't a dead end. It's a doorway. You are being guided through, gracefully and intentionally.

For Reflection

- Can you give yourself permission to feel the weight of the moment without losing sight of its temporary nature?
- What might your future self, the one who has come through this stronger, wiser, and whole, say to your current self?

5. YOUR EMERGENCE IS CERTAIN—IF YOU DON'T QUIT

> Let us not grow weary of doing good, for in due season we will reap, if we do not give up.
>
> —*Galatians 6:9 ESV*

Here's the promise: If you stay in the process, you will emerge.

Not maybe. Not if you're lucky. Not if everything aligns perfectly.

You will reap if you don't quit.

Galatians 6:9 uses the language of sowing and reaping. It's agricultural, but it's also spiritual. It reminds us that every step of faith, every moment of surrender, every ounce of trust in the cocoon is a seed, and seeds always produce.

Going into the cocoon is an act of sowing. You're sowing your comfort. You're sowing your certainty. You're sowing your expectations and your timeline and your desire to have it all figured out.

You're sowing the cost of surrender.

And the promise is that you will reap. Not because you forced the outcome, but because you stayed in the process. The breakthrough is already built into the process. Your only job is to not abandon the journey before the transformation is complete.

When you're in the cocoon, the temptation to quit is real. It feels like nothing is changing. It feels like you've been forgotten. It feels like the pressure will never lift. But those feelings are not the truth. The truth is that the moment you quit, you walk away from a harvest that was already on the way.

Your emergence is not a question of if, it's a matter of when.

Stay with it. The same God who started the work in you is faithful to complete it.

Takeaway

The cocoon works only if you stay inside long enough to be changed.

For Reflection

- Where in your life are you most tempted to quit, and what truth can you hold on to instead?

KNOWING FROM THE COCOON

The cocoon is not easy. It's not glamorous. It's not always inspirational. But it is divinely orchestrated. And now you know some things about the cocoon that perhaps you'd never considered before:

You know that God sees you—even here.
You know that you can trust his heart—even when his hand seems hidden.
You know that you are safe—even when you feel exposed.
You know that this won't last forever—even when it feels endless.

And now you know that your emergence is certain—if you just don't quit.

Knowing these truths won't remove the pain of the process. But it will anchor you in the midst of it. It will keep you grounded when everything around you is shifting. It will help you breathe when the air feels tight. And, most of all, it will remind you: You are not lost. You are becoming.

Let's keep going.

THE FOUNDATION OF KNOWING

The foundation of Knowing is found in a powerful passage of Scripture: "Be still, and know that I am God" (Ps. 46:10).

That word *still*, in its original language, carries the meaning "to cease, to stop, to let go." When you don't have a revelation of who God is—his power, his love, his faithfulness—you'll find yourself scrambling. Trying to figure out life on your own. Pushing, striving, fixing. It's exhausting. And it doesn't lead to peace. It eventually breaks down under the weight of your limitations.

But in this verse God is offering us something better. He's saying, *You can stop. You can rest. You don't have to carry this by yourself.* It's the same language used to describe Sabbath, where you cease not just from work but from worry. From control. From fear.

But there's a catch: The only way to truly rest is to know.

"Be still, and know that I am God."

Not just know facts about God but know his heart. Know his presence. Know that he *is*. That he is everything you need. That he is enough. It echoes what God told Moses when Moses asked, "Who should I say sent me?" God's answer? "I AM."

That phrase means more than just existence. It means God will be whatever he needs to be for his children. *I AM healer. I AM provider. I AM peace. I AM with you.*

There is a certainty that comes when you know the certainty of God. And when you know that, you can expect some things.

You can expect joy. James says, "Count it all joy when you fall into various trials" (1:2). Why? "Knowing that the testing of your faith produces . . ." (v. 3). Joy in trials is possible only because of what you know. When you know that trials produce endurance, maturity, and purpose, joy becomes a choice, not a reaction.

You can also expect optimism. Romans 8:28 says, "And we know that all things work together for good to those who love God, to those who are the called according to His purpose." There it is again: *We know.* Not we hope. Not we assume. We know. That kind of Knowing anchors our hope.

As I walked through my own cocoon, a season of uncertainty that pressed hard against my confidence, God began to lead me back to this foundation. He told me to still be joyful. To still be optimistic. And he led me right to these verses.

He also told me to stay in my daily rhythms and routines. To not allow the pressure of the cocoon to squeeze me into stillness that looks like defeat. To not disconnect. To keep showing up.

Joy is a choice. Optimism is a choice. And those choices become a lot easier when you know what you know.

That's what the cocoon taught me. Not just how to endure but how to be still in the middle of uncertainty and trust what I know when everything else feels unsure.

No matter where you find yourself today—in the dark, in the waiting, in the unraveling—be still. You are not forgotten. You are being formed. And if you stay with God in the process, you will not only survive it, you will emerge with a Knowing that cannot be shaken.

Earlier in this chapter I mentioned that my radical optimism had ghosted me.

Well, I'm happy to report it came back.

Not with an apology, not timidly, but with a wide grin and a deeper wisdom. And this time it didn't return alone. It brought with it something even more powerful than before: a deeper Knowing. A Knowing shaped by silence, struggle, and surrender. A Knowing built not on feelings but on truth.

I've emerged from this cocoon not just with renewed strength but with a message. And I'm ready now, more than ever, to take you on this journey. To walk with you into the deeper insights, blessings, and benefits of Knowing. Because I believe—with radical optimism—that what's ahead of you is greater than what's behind you.

And if you stay open, stay present, and stay grounded in truth, you'll find a version of yourself on the other side that's freer, stronger, and more faith-filled than you've ever known.

For Reflection

- If your cocoon could speak, what would it say?
- What truths are waiting for you in the silence?
- Write down what you're learning to know about God, about yourself, and about this season you're in.

EMERGING WITH KNOWING

The cocoon doesn't just change you, it teaches you. And if you've learned its lesson, you emerge not just healed but ready.

Ready to move forward with a bold, quiet certainty. A radical optimism. Not the kind that denies difficulty but the kind that has seen darkness and still believes in light.

That's the gift of the cocoon.

You exit with more than perspective. You exit with Knowing. Not just an idea. Not a feeling. But something deeper.

A sense.

A language.

A compass.

In the next chapter, we'll explore that inner faculty. The one that doesn't need to see to believe and doesn't need proof to proceed.

It's been with you all along.

And once you learn to trust it, you'll never walk the same again.

Let's take the next step, together.

TWO

THE FIRST SENSE

RETURNING TO YOUR KNOWING

IN THE PREVIOUS CHAPTER WE EXPLORED KNOWING as confidence, an inner assurance that steadies you when life unravels. It's the truth that holds when clarity disappears. The anchor you grip when everything familiar falls away. Knowing is your awareness of God, his nature, his nearness, and his unfailing promises. It is the soul's recognition of God's character, even when your circumstances seem to contradict it.

But Knowing doesn't stop there. As we peel back the layers, we see it not only as confidence but as something timeless and more essential. Beneath the steadiness it gives us in hard seasons, there is something even more foundational. Something ancient and alive.

Before Knowing became your anchor, it was your awareness. Before it helped you hold on, it helped you see. Not with your eyes but with your spirit.

This is the Knowing that existed before sight, before sound, before language. It is your first sense. The one you were born with. The quiet, intuitive recognition of God, of safety, of presence, of love, before you had words to name them. This kind of Knowing doesn't come through logic or education. It's woven into your being. It's how your soul recognizes truth without needing proof, whispering, "This is real. This is true. This is God."

And though we were created with it, we lost touch with it along the way. Life got loud. Pain made us question. Culture taught us to trust our senses, our logic, our plans, but not always our spirit. And so this first sense, the one that once came so naturally, grew faint.

But it's still there. Waiting. And this chapter is your invitation to return.

THE GENESIS OF KNOWING

I believe some of the profoundest truths are hidden in the simplest things. And too often we miss them. We've heard the story of creation so many times that it's easy to skim past it, as if it's a children's tale or a poetic prologue to the "real" parts of Scripture. But what if it's more than that? What if the creation account isn't just a history lesson but a blueprint? A memory? A mirror?

In the Genesis story, we don't just see how the world began. We see how we began. And more than that, we see how Knowing began. This first chapter of our human story is about more than light and land and animals. It is about the chemistry and symmetry between God and the ones made in his image. It is about the divine rhythm between creator and creation. It is about intimacy. Clarity. Connection. There was no fear. No shame. No confusion. Only presence. Only love. Only Knowing.

That is where Knowing began. Not as a concept. Not as information. But as communion. Before language, before law, before even need, there was God with us, and we knew him. This was humanity's original state. Knowing was not learned, it was lived.

When we reflect on the story of creation, we often focus on the poetry of it. The rhythm of the repeated phrase, "God said, 'Let there be . . .' and there was." We read those lines as if they are simply divine commands, echoing in an empty void, making things happen by force. And in a sense they are. But what we rarely consider is this: Who or what was on the other side of God's command? There was no audience. No listeners with ears. No witnesses with eyes. And yet there was a response. A happening. A becoming.

The Word was spoken, and creation knew what to do.

That's the mystery. There was no ear to hear, no brain to analyze, no interpreter nearby. Yet when God spoke, creation responded—not through the five senses but through something deeper. There was a transmission, a direct communion from Spirit to substance.

This pattern is echoed in the physical universe. At the fundamental level, matter responds to energy and frequency. Before there is form, there is resonance. Before there is sight, there is response. It's as if creation, from atoms to oceans, still remembers the sound of his voice.

And the same pattern lives in us. The first thing Adam experienced wasn't sight or touch; it was the breath of God filling his being (Gen. 2:7). That breath was more than life. It was awareness. Communion. Knowing. Even science nods to this mystery: Long before a newborn opens its eyes, it recognizes familiar voices, rhythms, and tones of love. Awareness precedes observation. We come into the world remembering before we learn.

Little glimpses of that memory still break through. Gentle nudges, sudden clarity, unexplainable peace. Neuroscientists call it intuition, those split-second impressions that seem to know before the mind can think. The heart and brain exchange subtle electrical signals, often registering truth before words form. It's as though the body itself still carries the echo of that first divine resonance, the residue of the moment God breathed awareness into dust.

And once you notice it, you realize this Knowing never left. It has simply been waiting to be remembered.

To live from this awareness is to see through God's eyes—to sense abundance where others see absence, and to perceive wholeness where others see lack. It's the same truth whispered through Scripture since the beginning.

Two passages speak directly to this idea—two of my favorites. And when you look at them through the lens of Knowing, something powerful unfolds.

The first is one we've heard countless times: "The LORD is my shepherd; I shall not want" (Ps. 23:1). But when you look at the original language, a more accurate rendering is this: "The LORD is my shepherd; I have no lack." This isn't just a statement of provision. It's a statement of perception.

David isn't saying that his Shepherd gave him everything he ever wanted. He's saying, "I'm so connected to my Shepherd that I don't even perceive lack." There is no anxiety, no scarcity, no chasing. There is trust. There is alignment. There is Knowing. He knows that everything he needs is already accounted for. That's the power of divine awareness. It changes how you see everything.

Then there's Psalm 37:4: "Delight yourself also in the LORD, and He shall give you the desires of your heart." We often read this and assume it means, "If I'm good and love God, he'll give me what I want." But that's not what the psalmist is saying. He's saying this: When you delight yourself in the Lord, when you build connection with him, he gives your heart *what to desire*. He doesn't just fulfill your desires. He forms them. He plants within you the very longings he intends to fulfill. And because they come from him, they will always lead to satisfaction.

This is the essence of divine Knowing: You no longer spend your life pursuing things that might fulfill you. You pursue what God has already appointed for you. And that's why your soul can rest.

I've been cultivating this kind of Knowing for a long time. And as we move further into this book, I'll be sharing many of the practical steps I took to get here. But I can tell you without hesitation: The extraordinary life I'm living now wasn't built because I'm the most intellectual person in the room. It wasn't because I came from money or privilege. I had a beautiful, loving family, but we weren't the Rockefellers. What we lacked in wealth we made up for in love.

It also wasn't because I had a wall full of degrees, or the perfect pedigree, or a network of powerful connections waiting to open every door.

The life I'm living today was built because I've spent years learning how to get better at listening—really listening—to what, deep down, I already knew.

That Knowing has guided everything.

- Making business moves that looked risky on the surface but turned out to be divinely timed
- Walking away from relationships that no longer aligned and stepping into new ones that breathed life into me
- Hiring the right people and releasing the wrong ones
- Making bold decisions others didn't understand, until the fruit began to speak for itself

If I had to sum it up, I'd say this: My entire life has been shaped by one thing: learning to lean in and trust the Knowing.

KNOWING IS IN THE STILLNESS

Knowing lives in the stillness. If you can get still enough, you will Know.

Throughout this book I'll often use *stillness* and *peace* interchangeably, because where one is, the other often follows. So let's talk about peace for a moment.

Peace is most often defined by what it isn't. It's the absence of conflict. The absence of war. The absence of anxiety or dissension. Which is interesting because that means we've come to understand peace by defining it against our dysfunction. We pursue it from a place of not having it, and, in doing so, we quietly accept that unrest is normal. That inner conflict is just part of life.

But that can't be what God intended.

It can't be in the divine design for wholeness to feel like a rare exception. It can't be God's plan that our baseline is chaos and our peace is a luxury.

The fact that peace feels foreign doesn't mean it's unnatural. It means we've strayed from what's original. In God's economy, peace isn't the exception, it's the expectation. It's the evidence of alignment. It's what fills the space where God dwells.

We'll return to that idea of conflict shortly. But first I want to point to a deeper meaning of peace.

In Hebrew, the word for peace is *shalom*. It doesn't just mean tranquility or quiet. Shalom means wholeness. It speaks of oneness—not just the absence of conflict but the presence of harmony, alignment, and unity. True peace, shalom, is the byproduct of our oneness with God. It's not just the stilling of our circumstances. It's the stilling of our soul through divine connection. And it is in that stillness, in that peace, that this Knowing I've been describing emerges.

In the year 2000 I had a dream that changed my life forever. It was the dream that God used to awaken me to my calling as a teacher of his Word. I won't go into all the details here. If you're curious, you can read more about it in my first book, *Purpose Awakening*. But there's one part I believe perfectly illustrates this idea of Knowing.

In the dream I was carried upward at an unspeakable speed. It felt like I was ascending at the speed of light. I was then thrust through a clear, fluidlike film, and, in an instant, the acceleration stopped. I arrived in a new dimension.

The first thing I noticed wasn't what I saw. It was what I felt. It was still. Peaceful. Quiet.

There was no anxiety. No striving. No confusion. There was only wholeness. Only presence. And in that place, I didn't just *have* knowledge, I was one with knowledge.

That's the best way I can describe it. It wasn't information being given to me. It was as though I had stepped into a dimension where I was already in union with truth. There was no separation between me and understanding. It was complete oneness.

What I didn't know at the time was that my dream aligned perfectly with a passage of Scripture in 1 Corinthians 13, where Paul writes, "Now I know in part; then I shall know fully, even as I am fully known" (1 Cor. 13:12 NIV). How powerful is that? To be so connected to God, to truth, to peace that you don't just receive knowledge, you become one with it.

That is what stillness makes room for. That is what peace unlocks. And that is what Knowing, your first sense, is always reaching to restore.

THE ORIGIN OF CONFUSION

Earlier I said I'd come back to the conflict—the internal disruption that robs us of the stillness, peace, and oneness with God that brings us into Knowing. Let's talk about it.

Here's the premise I want to establish: Stillness is not the absence of noise. It's much deeper than that. Stillness comes when the disruptor, and its residue, has been subdued. So the questions become, What disruptor? and When did the disruption begin?

It began in the garden, at the very beginning of the human story.

The first humans were in total communion with God. Their connection with him was unbroken. The flow of divine awareness, the Knowing, was uninterrupted. What God knew, they received.

What God said, they trusted. There was no confusion, no fear, no doubt. The Knowing flowed freely from God's Spirit to their souls.

But then a voice entered the story. A deceiver in the form of a serpent.

The serpent didn't use violence. He didn't need to. He used suggestion. He subtly sowed a single dangerous idea: that the source of their Knowing wasn't trustworthy.

"Did God really say . . . ?" With that one question, the clarity of communion was pierced by doubt.

The Enemy's strategy wasn't simply to tempt them with knowledge. It was to disconnect them from the flow of Knowing by making them distrust the one who was giving it. And the moment divine truth became negotiable, confusion entered. When the Enemy's lie became their logic, the Knowing stopped flowing.

What followed wasn't just a moral misstep, it was a spiritual disconnection. A fracture in the frequency. They went from walking in union to hiding in shame. From being naked and unashamed to covering what was once uncovered. From knowing God effortlessly to questioning him instinctively.

This is where the conflict began. And this is the root of the unrest we still feel today. The disconnection that happened in the garden wasn't a onetime event. It's still happening, every day, in our lives, in our culture, in our decisions. We may not call it by name, but we feel it.

It looks like striving without peace. It looks like hustling for worth, chasing clarity, constantly refreshing our feeds while our souls feel foggier and foggier. It looks like a dependence on what we can see, touch, measure, and manage while we quietly wonder, *Why does it still not feel like enough?*

It looks like running toward success only to arrive and feel the ache of *Is this all there is?* It looks like the person who has all the degrees, all the connections, all the boxes checked and yet wakes up anxious because something inside still feels untethered. It looks like overthinking every decision, second-guessing your instincts, mistrusting the quiet voice within because somewhere along the way, you stopped believing that *you* could know.

It looks like religion without relationship. Achievement without alignment. Noise without peace. Knowledge without Knowing.

We've become masters of information and strangers to divine awareness.

But this was never God's design. Confusion was never meant to be our home. Disconnection was never meant to be our normal.

The disconnection we inherited through our stumble in the garden shows up every time we forget who we are and, more important, *whose* we are. Every time we trust what we see over what God says. Every time we choose fear over faith, striving over surrender, doubt over the quiet certainty of his presence.

But the beauty is this: What was lost can be recovered.

THE WAY BACK TO KNOWING

But there was a twist in the story. A twist the Enemy didn't see coming.

The one who knows all things had a plan. Not a reaction. Not a spiritual plan B. But a strategy that existed from the very beginning. Before the mistake, before the disconnection, there was already a way to bring humanity back into alignment. Back to peace. Back to presence. Back to Knowing. "The Lamb slain from the foundation of the world" (Rev. 13:8).

Before we ever lost our way, God had already made a way. That strategy had a name: Jesus.

Long before history recorded him, he existed. Long before the pain, the confusion, the noise, the striving, there was a way already prepared. Jesus wasn't sent to start a religion. He came to restore what was lost. To bring us back to the divine awareness we were created for. To reconnect us to the voice we were always meant to trust. To silence the lies of the Enemy that first broke our sense of clarity. "The reason the Son of God appeared was to destroy the works of the devil" (1 John 3:8 ESV). He came to destroy the confusion. To undo the damage. To reintroduce us to God, not as a distant deity, but as a loving Father who never stopped reaching for his children.

And here's the beautiful part: Jesus didn't just come to put things back the way they were. He came to lead us into something even greater. A relationship marked by clarity. A life built on truth. A rhythm of living where Knowing becomes natural again. Not something rare or mysterious but something familiar, accessible, and steady.

The way back to Knowing has always been open. And now, through Jesus, it's ours to walk in.

Jesus once said something fascinating about himself: "My sheep hear My voice, and I know them, and they follow Me" (John 10:27). He was describing a relationship. Rooted not in religion or ritual but in recognition.

"They know my voice." Not "They study my words" or "They memorize my commands" but "They know." They recognize the sound of him. They're tuned in. Aligned. Aware.

And just as powerfully, he said, "They will never follow a stranger . . . because they do not recognize a stranger's voice" (v. 5 NIV). When you know Jesus, you become less susceptible to confusion. You begin to sense what is him and what isn't. You become familiar with the frequency of truth. But Jesus didn't just teach this, he modeled it.

When questioned about the legitimacy of what he was doing, he said, "The Son can do nothing of Himself, but what He sees the Father do" (John 5:19).

In another place, he said, "I do nothing on my own but speak just what the Father has taught me" (John 8:28 NIV).

Jesus lived in complete awareness of his Father's presence. He listened. He watched. He followed. He showed us what it looks like to live a life led by Knowing, a life marked by divine awareness and daily connection.

That's what he came to restore. He came not only to offer forgiveness and salvation but also to restore in us a deep, relational awareness of God's voice.

There is nothing more profound than that. One of the greatest gifts of following Jesus is the ability to hear and perceive the voice of God. That's not reserved for prophets, preachers, or "super spiritual" people. That's an invitation for all of us.

This is the essence of Knowing. Not merely believing that God exists but walking with him. Listening. Trusting. Recognizing his voice in a world full of noise. And following him, not blindly but with confidence, because you know him.

WORSHIP IS THE WAY BACK

All throughout Scripture we're encouraged to seek: Seek wisdom. Seek the kingdom. Seek the Lord.

But there's one place in Scripture where we're told what *God* is seeking.

In Jesus' conversation with a woman at a well—a woman thirsty not just for water but for truth, healing, and restoration—he reveals something divine and intimate. He tells her what the Almighty is after. Not sacrifice. Not perfection. Not performance. The Father is seeking "true worshipers." Those who "will worship the Father in spirit and truth" (John 4:23).

I've come to understand that worship is not about a song, though songs can carry it. Worship is not a building, though sacred spaces can hold it. Worship is about oneness. More specifically, worship is about oneness with the God who created you. It's about intimacy. And you can't have intimacy without Knowing.

There's a Hebrew word for "know": *yada*. It doesn't just mean intellectual awareness. It speaks of deep, personal, experiential intimacy. In several places in Scripture *yada* is used to describe the most intimate human experience. "Now Adam knew Eve his wife, and she conceived and bore Cain" (Gen. 4:1). This wasn't about information, it was about union. Worship is spiritual *yada*. It's the opening of your heart, your soul, your mind, your entire being into divine connection.

Have you ever seen someone in a moment of pure worship? Arms stretched wide, head tilted back, eyes closed, a look of peace and joy resting on their face. It's not a performance. It's a posture. It looks like someone being held, because, in a very real way, they are.

If you strip away the sensual elements of human intimacy and consider its essence—openness, union, surrender—you start to understand what happens when we worship. We open ourselves and God enters in. He completes what's missing. There's an exchange: His wholeness for our brokenness. His peace for our anxiety. His strength for our weakness.

But here's the most transformative exchange of all: his image for ours.

When we worship, we behold God face to face. And as we behold him, we are transformed into that same image. We begin to reflect what we've been looking at. We become one. "And we all, who with unveiled faces contemplate the Lord's glory, are being transformed into his image with ever-increasing glory" (2 Cor. 3:18 NIV).

There's a mystery here that we can't overlook.

Paul is telling us that transformation doesn't come from effort, it comes from beholding. The more we behold God, the more we begin to reflect him. It's not about striving to become holy. It's about staring at holiness until it starts staring back at us.

This is the supernatural power of worship: It positions us to behold. Not to analyze. Not to figure out. But to gaze. To lock eyes with the one who made us. And in that gaze, in that sacred exchange, we change.

This is why the Knowing flows so freely in worship. Because when you see clearly, you know deeply.

Have you ever noticed how couples who've been together for years begin to look alike? Or how they can communicate without speaking, finish each other's sentences, feel what the other is feeling? My wife, Sarah, and I know that kind of flow. We can glance at each other in the middle of a crowded room and have an entire conversation without words. That's Knowing. And it's been cultivated over years of intimacy. That's what worship creates between us and God. Not just belief. Not just reverence. But oneness. And in that oneness, Knowing is restored.

RETURNING TO YOUR KNOWING

If you've made it this far, you're probably starting to feel what this chapter has been building toward not just in your mind but in your heart. Not just a new idea but a deeper awareness. A quiet remembering. A stirring.

We began this chapter with a bold claim: that Knowing is not the sixth sense, it's the first. It's not something we grow into. It's something we were born with. And even though life may have dulled it, distracted us from it, disconnected us from it, it was never lost. It's been waiting for us to return.

We explored what it looks like to live without that Knowing, chasing what we already have, longing for what we were made for, settling for noise when we were designed for clarity. But Jesus—Jesus is the way back.

He came not just to save us but to restore us. To reconnect us to the voice we were always meant to trust. To lead us back into communion. Intimacy. Wholeness. And through worship, he invites us into oneness, where Knowing flows freely again.

So if you're sensing something happening in your heart right now—that quiet awareness, that stirring beneath the surface—that's not emotion. That's Knowing. It's the first sense coming alive again. And I want to invite you to respond to it. Not with performance. Not with striving. But with openness. Let the Restorer in. The one who came to destroy the works of the Enemy. So that you can be whole again. So that you can Know again.

Well, my friend, this is only the beginning. There is still so much to discover. So much to remember. Because Knowing isn't just a feeling. It's a way of living. And in the next part of this journey, we're going to get practical.

Together, we will learn how to listen. How to discern. How to make decisions from a deeper place. How to build a life on what you know even when you can't yet see it.

Let's keep going. There's more waiting for you. More Knowing to come.

THREE

UNKNOWING

REBUILDING THE TEMPLE OF THE MIND

IF YOU'VE MADE IT THIS FAR, I ALREADY KNOW SOMEthing about you: You're hungry. You're searching. And maybe, just maybe, something deep inside you is starting to remember.

You've been walking through the early parts of this book not just reading but reflecting. You've paused midsentence. You've highlighted things that felt too true to ignore. You've wrestled. You've nodded. You've felt the pull. That's not just curiosity. That's Knowing waking back up. And I want to celebrate that.

Because this isn't a linear journey. It's a spiral. We don't just move forward. We move deeper. And the deeper we go, the more we uncover, not just about God but about ourselves.

In the previous chapter we remembered that Knowing was our first sense. A divine awareness that connected us to God before we had words. We learned that it wasn't lost, just buried under noise, culture, pain, and fear. And we saw that Jesus came not just to rescue us but to restore us to that original state of intimacy, peace, and Knowing.

But as many of us are beginning to realize that restoration doesn't happen all at once. It's not a light switch. It's a rebuilding process.

And every rebuilding begins with a teardown.

Because as beautiful as Knowing is, there's something that often stands in its way: what we think we know. The stories we've inherited. The lies we've believed. The mental frameworks we've built around survival, not surrender.

You see, the damage done in the garden didn't just leave us

spiritually disconnected, it also reshaped our minds. And if Knowing is to flourish again, it has to happen there. Right where the confusion started. Right in the temple of our thoughts. "With my mind I serve the Law of God" (Rom. 7:25 CEV). Which is why this chapter isn't just about learning. It's about unknowing. Letting go of what never belonged. Making space for what was always meant to live in you.

This is the work. It's sacred. It's necessary. And it's where your deeper Knowing takes root.

Unknowing isn't about losing something. It's about making room. Room for clarity. Room for truth. Room for a deeper kind of Knowing to rise again. In the next several sections, I want to walk with you through that process, layer by layer, belief by belief. Let's begin where every transformation starts: with the courage to question.

THE COURAGE TO QUESTION

There's a quiet kind of courage that doesn't always look brave from the outside. It's the courage to question. Not just to question the world around you but to question the beliefs within you. To ask, Why do I believe this? Where did this come from? And is it still serving me?

That kind of courage came for me in waves. During my first serious relationship with my college sweetheart, who later became my wife and the mother of my children, I believed I had found what every person is searching for: love, purpose, a future. We were both good people. We wanted the right things. We were building a life together. And for a while, it seemed like enough.

But over the course of our seventeen-year journey, things

shifted. We separated and reconciled more than once, each time hoping that prayer, counseling, retreats, or renewed commitment would make it whole. But the cracks were getting deeper and more undeniable.

It wasn't until a final counseling session—a last-ditch effort—that the truth finally surfaced. It wasn't a bolt of lightning, it was a slow unraveling. A quiet realization that knocked the wind out of me. The revelation was this: What brought us together wasn't love in its purest form, it was my brokenness. And now that healing had become my personal mandate, that foundation could no longer hold.

I nearly ran out of that counseling office just to keep from falling apart.

It's one thing to suffer. It's another to realize that your suffering might have a story behind it you were never taught to question. But questioning isn't betrayal. It's the beginning of rebuilding. And it's the doorway back to Knowing.

When you start asking why—why you think this way, why you tolerate what you do, why certain patterns repeat—you're not being difficult. You're being brave.

Scripture tells us it's with our minds that we serve the Lord, which means that if the Enemy can shape our thinking, he can shape our direction. That's why it matters to question what shaped your beliefs in the first place. Were they rooted in truth? Or were they born in environments of fear, dysfunction, or survival? To return to Knowing, we must first acknowledge that some of what we "know" was shaped by dysfunction, not divine wisdom.

This section of the journey isn't about being right. It's about being real. It's about saying, "Maybe I need to reexamine the blueprint before I keep building." That's where unknowing begins. Not with shame. Not with regret. But with the courage to question, so we can return to what's true.

For Reflection

- What have you accepted as truth that might actually be fear in disguise?
- Where in your life do you feel the quiet nudge to question? Not to deconstruct for the sake of destruction but to make room for Knowing to flow again?

THE FREEDOM OF LETTING GO

There's a moment in every journey when the truth becomes too loud to ignore. Not in an aggressive or punishing way but in a way that liberates you. It's the moment you realize, *I can't carry this and become who I'm called to be.*

For me, the moment came inside that counseling room.

As I mentioned before, it was one of my final attempts to save what had already begun to unravel. We seriously tried everything—prayer, retreats, therapy, even rigid religious commitments. But this time was different. Somewhere in the middle of that session a truth emerged that shifted everything. Not because it was brand-new but because I was finally still enough to hear it.

Without going into detail, I can tell you that what was uncovered wasn't malicious. It wasn't dramatic. It was just true. And it unraveled me.

In that moment, I saw something I had never fully admitted: The bond we'd built had been shaped more by need than by clarity. It was rooted in who we were trying to become, not in who we actually were. And as I stepped more fully into healing, it became clear that the foundation we stood on could no longer support the future I was being called to build.

Letting go didn't feel brave. It felt like grief. It felt like failure. It felt like the death of something I thought would last forever.

But here's what I've come to understand: Letting go isn't always an act of weakness. Sometimes it's the most courageous, most obedient, most Knowing thing you can do.

Letting go doesn't mean dishonoring the past. It means making peace with it. It means creating space for what's next. It means releasing what no longer serves the truth that's rising within you. In the economy of God, surrender is never about loss. It's about alignment. And alignment is where clarity flows.

What I couldn't see then but know now is that every release was making room. Room for new vision. Room for deeper peace. Room for the next version of me to emerge.

Letting go is not the end. It's the threshold.

For Reflection

- What are you holding on to that may have been built in brokenness rather than wholeness?
- Is there something in your life that served a purpose once but no longer fits where you're going?

THE ROLE OF UNLEARNING IN TRANSFORMATION

Letting go is just the beginning. Once you release what no longer fits, something else begins to happen. A quiet space opens up inside you. And with that space comes the next invitation: unlearning.

Unlearning gets a bad reputation. It sounds like forgetting. It sounds like failure. But in reality, unlearning is one of the most important parts of growth.

After my marriage ended, I found myself walking through a landscape I didn't recognize. Not just emotionally but mentally. I was questioning everything: my choices, my expectations, my beliefs about love, healing, wholeness, even God's plan for my life. And at first I felt guilty for those questions. But over time I realized it wasn't faithlessness. It was freedom. I was being invited to unlearn. To unlearn the beliefs I built from pain. To unlearn the roles I thought I had to play. To unlearn the patterns I accepted as normal but that were never aligned with who I was. Transformation doesn't begin when you get something new. It begins when you release what never belonged.

That's the hard truth of unlearning: Sometimes what needs to go isn't toxic or obviously destructive. Sometimes it's just outdated. Too small for the version of you that's emerging. No longer aligned with what you now know to be true. Scripture says, "Be transformed by the renewing of your mind" (Rom. 12:2). That word *renewing* in its original Greek means "to renovate." Which means this passage isn't merely describing inspiration, it is describing construction. To renovate the mind is to clear out what's old, outdated, or misaligned and make space for something truer, stronger, and more lasting to be built in its place.

The verse continues to express the idea that only by renewing your mind can you begin to "prove what is that good and acceptable and perfect will of God." You can't fully walk in what God has envisioned for your life until your mind becomes a place where his truth can live. This is why the temple metaphor matters. The mind is not just where thoughts live. It's where vision is sharpened. It's where clarity is cultivated. It's where purpose is made plain.

Unlearning is not a loss. It's a return. A remembering. It's a way of saying, "I trust God enough to update my beliefs."

And transformation begins right there.

For Reflection

- Can you think of a moment when clarity came not because you gained something new but because you let go of something false?
- Is there a belief you've accepted about God, yourself, or your future that you now sense is too small?

THE REFRAMING OF IDENTITY

One of the most unexpected outcomes of unlearning is the way it clears the mirror.

You start to see yourself more clearly. Not through the eyes of trauma, culture, expectation, or fear but through the eyes of the one who created you. And what you begin to see is not someone broken but someone becoming.

After my divorce there was a season when I genuinely didn't know who I was anymore. So much of my identity had been wrapped up in the roles I played. Husband. Father. Pastor. CEO. Provider. I had built my sense of self around those roles, and when one of them was disrupted, it felt like all of them were suddenly in question.

But here's what I discovered on the other side of that breakdown: Those roles weren't the problem. The problem was that I had mistaken my roles for my identity.

It's easy to confuse the two, especially when you're good at carrying them. But eventually life will bring you to a place where the mask no longer fits. Where the performance becomes too heavy. Where the truth pushes through the cracks. And it's in that place—raw, exposed, uncertain—that God reintroduces you to yourself. Not the version shaped by pressure or religion or image. The true you. The one that was formed in his mind before you ever took a breath.

This is the reframing of identity.

It's not about starting from scratch but about returning to the blueprint. It's about stripping away what was projected onto you and reclaiming what was placed *within* you.

You are not what happened to you. You are not who you had to become just to survive. You are not limited to the version of yourself that other people could understand. You are who God says you are. And as the old mental framework falls away, what rises in its place is someone who is whole. Someone who was always known. Someone who Knows.

This is the version of you that was always waiting to be seen.

For Reflection

- Are there parts of yourself you've hidden to fit into someone else's vision of who you should be?
- In what ways have you mistaken what you do for who you are?

TRUST IN THE PROCESS OF UNKNOWING

There's a moment in every transformation when you feel suspended. You've let go of what was but haven't yet arrived at what will be. You've released the old frameworks, but the new ones haven't fully taken shape. And in that space it's tempting to panic.

But this in-between place is not a mistake. It's part of the process.

The work of unknowing can feel disorienting. When you start stripping away false identities, old belief systems, and inherited ideas of truth, you may feel like you've lost your footing. But what you're actually losing is the illusion of stability, so you can finally root yourself in something real.

That feeling of groundlessness is not failure. It's freedom starting to stretch its legs.

There was a time in my own journey when I questioned everything I thought I knew. I had unraveled so much that it felt like nothing familiar remained, not even me. But looking back now, I can see that I wasn't falling apart. I was falling into truth.

You see, Knowing isn't always immediate. Sometimes it unfolds slowly, like a sunrise—soft at first, then suddenly undeniable. And in the meantime what God asks of us is to trust. Trust that what you've released needed to go. Trust that what's being rebuilt is rooted in him. Trust that this unfamiliar version of you is not lost, it's becoming.

To know God is to trust his pace. To trust that even when your understanding lags behind, his presence is already there. Trust that even when you can't see clearly, the first sense is still alive inside you, leading you back to alignment, back to peace, back to Knowing. Because Knowing isn't a destination. It's a way of walking. And this is part of that walk.

So breathe. You're not broken. You're being rebuilt.

And what's on the other side of this unknowing is not just clarity, it's communion. It's not just new knowledge. It's a deeper, truer, more embodied Knowing than you've ever had before.

Sometimes the most defining ground is the space between letting go and rising up. The quiet place where your old thoughts are silent and your new ones have yet to speak. But even here you are not alone. Even here something is being formed in you. A strength. A soundness. A strategy.

When God begins to rebuild the temple of your mind, he does not leave you unarmed. He gives you tools. He gives you truth. He gives you the power to tear down what was never meant to stand. And now it's time to fight for your mind. Not with fear. But with fortitude. With boldness. With Knowing.

For Reflection

- What emotions are rising as you let go of old beliefs or identities? Can you name them without judging them?
- How might your life change if you chose to trust the unfolding instead of trying to control it?
- What would it look like to believe that even in the fog your Knowing is still present and guiding you?

SECURING THE TERRITORY OF THE MIND

If the mind is the temple, then our thoughts are the territory. And that territory is constantly being contested.

Not always loudly. Not always obviously. But quietly. Subtly. In the form of beliefs we've inherited, identities we've accepted, and internal narratives we've never dared to question.

This is where the process of unknowing reaches a new level. While some beliefs can be released with reflection or revelation, others are entrenched. They've been reinforced for so long—by pain, by repetition, by culture, even by religion—that they've taken on structure.

In 2 Corinthians 10:4–5, Paul calls these entrenched patterns strongholds. And in the original Greek, that word paints a picture: a fortress. A castle. "The weapons we fight with are not the weapons of the world. On the contrary, they have divine power to demolish strongholds. We demolish arguments and every pretension that sets itself up against the knowledge of God, and we take captive every thought to make it obedient to Christ" (NIV). Strongholds are not just thoughts. They are fortified arguments. Defensive systems built into our thinking. Thought patterns so reinforced that we can no longer tell where the truth ends and the lie begins. They protect falsehoods that feel like facts. They house beliefs we don't even know we're living by.

That's why this part of the journey is so critical. This is not just about letting go of what no longer serves you. It's about confronting what's been serving you lies for years and replacing it with truth.

This is the heart of unknowing: Not just subtracting beliefs but dismantling strongholds. Not just clearing space but taking back ground. Not just questioning lies but building altars of truth in their place. Because here's what Scripture reveals: We are not just casting down random thoughts. We are tearing down anything that exalts itself against the knowledge of Christ.

And what is the knowledge of Christ? It is Knowing. It is divine awareness restored. It is the very thing Jesus came to bring back into the human experience. The abiding awareness of who God is, who we are in him, and what's possible when we live from that place.

This is the knowledge of Christ that silences shame. That heals identity. That calls lies by name and replaces them with grace. This is the restored Knowing we've been journeying toward from the beginning of this book.

Jesus came to destroy the works of the Enemy—yes. But he also came to restore our access to what I call Divine Intelligence. He came to renew the mind, recalibrate the soul, and rebuild the inner sanctuary where truth can dwell.

And that is where we're headed next.

In the next chapter, we'll explore what it means to live from the knowledge of Christ. Not as a theological idea but as a source of wisdom, discernment, clarity, and supernatural insight. We'll learn how to access what Jesus died to give us: a mind fully aligned with heaven and a Knowing that never wavers.

You've questioned. You've released. You've unlearned. You've reframed. You've reclaimed.

Now the temple is ready. The mind is clear. What comes next is Divine Intelligence.

FOUR

DIVINE INTELLIGENCE

ARTIFICIAL INTELLIGENCE HAS TAKEN THE WORLD BY storm, and for good reason. It's fast. It's efficient. It can process more information in seconds than a human mind can in days. It's changing the way we work, communicate, and even create. Whether you're using it to generate ideas, optimize business systems, or streamline communication, AI is without question one of the most revolutionary innovations of our time.

I talked about this very thing on my podcast, *The Called*, in an episode titled "Why Teams, Tools, and Training Matter." I shared how, if you're not integrating some form of AI into your life or business, you're not just behind, you're at risk of being left behind. Your competitors are gaining ground. And you're missing the boat entirely.

Yes, AI has sparked controversy. Yes, there are valid concerns. But what no one can deny is that artificial intelligence, when used with wisdom, is a tool of tremendous advantage.

Yet as powerful as it is, AI is still limited. Because AI, for all its speed and brilliance, is only as good as the information it's given. It can gather. It can organize. But it cannot originate. It cannot create Knowing. It can only reflect what has already been said.

There is, however, another kind of intelligence. One that doesn't process information. It *is* information. One that doesn't just respond to the data. It *was* the data before time began.

This is what I call Divine Intelligence. And Divine Intelligence puts artificial intelligence to shame.

Divine Intelligence is not powered by algorithms. It is powered by the Spirit of the living God. It is perfect knowledge. Timeless wisdom. Infinite perspective. It's not something you build, it's something you receive. It's not something you program, it's something you perceive. It's the intelligence behind creation itself, and it's the foundation of Knowing.

Artificial intelligence may help you move faster. Divine Intelligence helps you move in purpose. AI can give you an edge. Divine Intelligence gives you direction. AI can sort what's already known. Divine Intelligence reveals what no one else sees.

And here's the best part: It's available to you—right now.

In this chapter we will explore what Divine Intelligence is, how it flows, and how to access it. Because you were never meant to navigate life with just information. You were designed to walk with divine Knowing.

Let's begin.

THE MIND OF GOD

Divine Intelligence is not a mystical superpower reserved for a spiritual elite. It's not locked behind religious performance or theological degrees. It's a gift. A promise. An open invitation to anyone willing to receive it.

This isn't just my perspective, it's straight from Scripture.

In 1 Corinthians 2, Paul makes an extraordinary claim. He tells us that we have access to the thoughts of God, not someday in heaven but here and now, through his Spirit.

> But we speak the wisdom of God in a mystery, the hidden wisdom which God ordained before the ages for our glory, which none of the rulers of this age knew; for had they known, they would not have crucified the Lord of glory.

> But as it is written:
>
> "Eye has not seen, nor ear heard,
> Nor have entered into the heart of man
> The things which God has prepared for those who love Him."
>
> But God has revealed them to us through His Spirit. For the Spirit searches all things, yes, the deep things of God.
>
> —*1 Corinthians 2:7–10*

Take that in for a moment. What no one has seen. What no one has heard. What no one has imagined. God has already revealed, through his Spirit.

And Paul doesn't stop there:

> For the Spirit searches all things, yes, the deep things of God. For what man knows the things of a man except the spirit of the man which is in him? Even so no one knows the things of God except the Spirit of God. Now we have received . . . the Spirit who is from God, that we might know the things that have been freely given to us by God.
>
> —*vv. 10–12*

This is the biblical foundation for Divine Intelligence.

Through the Spirit of God, we've been given access to what he wants us to know. Not just about him but from him. This is not generic wisdom. This is specific revelation, made available through divine connection.

But let me be clear: This kind of access is not automatic. To receive Divine Intelligence, we must also be willing to receive the Spirit of God. And if that's something you haven't yet experienced—if you're unsure whether you've received the Spirit—we're going to walk through that together later. Because this level of Knowing isn't reserved for the gifted. It's available to the willing.

The same Spirit that searched the depths of God and revealed them to Paul is still active today. Still speaking. Still revealing. Still making known the things that have been freely given to us by God.

You don't have to guess your way forward. You don't have to walk blindly or rely only on logic. Divine Intelligence is real. It's alive. And it's how you were always meant to live. Not just informed but aligned. Not just learning but Knowing.

And here's what makes that Knowing even more extraordinary: "Now He who searches the hearts knows what the mind of the Spirit is, because He makes intercession for the saints according to the will of God" (Rom. 8:27). This is the Spirit's role. Not only to reveal the mind of God but to search our hearts. To close the gap between God's will and our awareness. To make sure that what God wants to reveal isn't just spoken but received. That what God knows isn't just available but known.

Divine Intelligence is the Spirit of God searching the deep things of God and the hidden places in us until the two come into alignment.

And from that alignment everything changes.

In the next section, we're going to explore how to access this kind of intelligence. You'll learn how to open yourself to the Spirit, how to create space for divine insight to flow, and how to begin walking in the kind of Knowing that was always meant to guide your life.

THE SPIRIT OF KNOWING

If Divine Intelligence is made available to us through the Spirit of God, then the next question becomes, How do we access it?

To answer that, we have to look to Jesus.

Not just Jesus the teacher or miracle worker but Jesus the friend, as he shared a final meal with his disciples, knowing his time with them was short. These were the ones who had walked closely with him. They had heard his voice. Watched his every move. But he knew their connection to divine truth couldn't depend on proximity alone.

So in one of the most intimate moments of his ministry, he makes a promise that shocks his disciples. He tells them he's going, but someone else is coming. Not a replacement but a continuation. And seeing how upsetting his departure will be to them, Jesus offers a reassurance that still stretches the imagination: "It's better for you that I go."

He compels them to realize that it will indeed be better for them if he leaves. Better than having him physically present. Better than walking with him, talking with him, asking him questions face to face.

Why?

Because his leaving will make room for something—and someone—that will change everything. "Unless I go away, the Advocate will not come to you; but if I go, I will send him to you" (John 16:7 NIV). Depending on your translation, Jesus also calls him the Comforter. The Helper. The Encourager. But make no mistake, he is talking about the Holy Spirit.

Jesus also says something even more staggering: "He will teach you all things" (John 14:26). All things. Not some things. Not just spiritual things. All things.

That's Divine Intelligence.

And guess who he is talking to? Not a handful of spiritual elites. Not scholars or prophets. He is talking to his disciples—ordinary people like you and me.

Jesus knew something we often forget: Information is not enough. Even after walking with him for three years, the disciples were not yet ready. Not until they received the Spirit. Not until Divine Intelligence entered the building.

That's why he tells them not to move. Not to preach. Not to build. Not to launch into their calling. Not to pursue their purpose. "Tarry in the city of Jerusalem until you are endued with power from on high" (Luke 24:49). Because calling without clarity is dangerous. Purpose without power is exhausting. And movement without guidance is just busyness.

Jesus makes it clear: You cannot walk in what you're called to do without the Holy Spirit.

The Spirit of God is not just a presence you feel. He is the revealer of Knowing. The searcher of the deep things of God. The guide into *all* truth. The voice of heaven echoing inside your being. The fulfillment of Jesus' promise to bring the mind of God into your everyday life.

So if you've ever wondered how to access Divine Intelligence, this is how it begins.

ACCESSING DIVINE INTELLIGENCE

Now, if you're expecting a complex theological breakdown for how to access Divine Intelligence, how to unlock the mind of God, decode mysteries, and receive heavenly downloads, you might want to take a seat.

Because here it is: Just ask.

That's it.

No formula. No spiritual gymnastics. No perfect track record required.

Jesus makes it clear in one of his most generous and jaw-dropping teachings about the Holy Spirit in Luke 11. He's talking to a group of people who have all kinds of needs, some named, some not. And instead of listing every possible situation they might face, he goes straight to the heart.

He describes a Father. Not a distant one. Not a complicated one. But a good one. One who loves to give. One who responds when his children come close. "Ask and it will be given to you; seek and you will find; knock and the door will be opened to you" (Luke 11:9 NIV). But it's what Jesus says next that unlocks everything: "If you then, though you are evil, know how to give good gifts to your children, how much more will your Father in heaven give the Holy Spirit to those who ask him!" (v. 13 NIV).

Wait—did you catch that? Jesus doesn't say, "How much more will the Father give you solutions—money, healing, direction, power." Even though we might ask for those things, he names the Holy Spirit as the answer to all of it.

Because when you have the Spirit, you have the source. You have access to wisdom, peace, power, revelation—Knowing. Everything you could ever need is already present in him. So whatever your need is today, God's answer may not always be a blueprint. It may be a person: the Spirit of Knowing. And all you have to do is ask.

But how you ask matters.

James puts it plainly: "But let him ask in faith, with no doubting, for he who doubts is like a wave of the sea driven and tossed by the wind. For let not that man suppose that he will receive anything from the Lord" (1:6–7). Asking in faith means trusting in who you're asking. That God is good. That he gives without hesitation. That it's his good pleasure to give you all things, not reluctantly but lovingly.

So the next time you feel stuck or unsure, in need of guidance, you don't have to strive. You don't have to beg. You don't have to be perfect. You just have to be positioned, in faith, with a heart open to receive. Because Divine Intelligence doesn't begin with your performance. It begins with your posture.

Just ask.

But here's the wild thing about asking: Sometimes we don't even know what to ask for. What we need most might already be in our possession. We just haven't recognized it yet.

When we received Jesus, we were given more than we understood in that moment. Within us are hidden wisdom and potential, planted by God, woven into our spirit, ready to be revealed.

And part of the journey of Divine Intelligence is learning to discover what's already within.

DIVINE LANGUAGE

Receiving Jesus is only the beginning. Unpacking what he gives us is a lifelong discovery.

Yes, we receive forgiveness. Grace. New life. But along with that comes access. Power. And intelligence. And one of the greatest challenges we'll face as believers is simply learning to understand what we already have.

Paul understood this tension. Writing to a group of new believers in Ephesus, he prays that the eyes of their understanding will be enlightened, "that you may know what is the hope of His calling, what are the riches of the glory of His inheritance in the saints" (Eph. 1:18). In other words: You already have it. Now you need to see it. There is an inheritance—rich, layered, powerful—waiting to be explored. And one of the most significant, yet often misunderstood, parts of that inheritance is what I call divine language.

UNDERSTANDING DIVINE LANGUAGE

Some call it heavenly language. Others call it speaking in tongues. Some call it gibberish. And others believe it is a thing of the past. I'm not here to argue with anyone about their interpretation. We all walk out our faith in stages, and with sensitivity to how God works uniquely in us.

But I can tell you this from personal experience: Divine language has changed my life.

Not because I needed to prove I had the Holy Spirit. Truthfully, I experienced the wisdom, guidance, boldness, and inner Knowing of the Spirit long before I ever spoke or prayed in my heavenly language. But when that part of my inheritance was activated, something shifted. A new depth opened up. A new flow of joy, power, and spiritual vitality came alive in me. And it continues to this day.

Paul writes in 1 Corinthians 14 that the one who speaks in an unknown tongue "edifies himself" (v. 4). The word *edify* is architectural. It means to be built up, strengthened, reinforced. When I pray in divine language, I can feel that edification. It's as if my spirit is being restructured from the inside out.

But there's more.

Romans 8 says: "The Spirit also helps in our weaknesses. For we do not know what we should pray for as we ought, but the Spirit Himself makes intercession for us with groanings which cannot be uttered" (Rom. 8:26). Now, don't misunderstand that word *weakness*. Paul isn't just talking about a personal flaw, he's talking about our human limitations. We were created to walk in divine Knowing. But in our humanity, there are moments when we don't know what to pray, what to decide, or how to move forward. And in those moments, the Spirit prays for us, through us, with Divine Intelligence.

And here's something I want to make sure you don't miss. Paul also says that when we pray in divine language, we speak mysteries. There are things happening in the spiritual realm, things beyond our natural perception, that are being addressed in perfect alignment with God's will. "For anyone who speaks in a tongue does not speak to people but to God. Indeed, no one understands them; they utter mysteries by the Spirit" (1 Cor. 14:2 NIV).

Mysteries.

There are things happening in the spirit realm that cannot be accessed through logic, intellect, or emotion. They can be accessed only through Knowing. And sometimes that Knowing is so deep, so essential, that it bypasses human understanding entirely.

That's what divine language makes possible. You are not just speaking, you are unlocking. Praying things you don't yet understand. Touching things you may never see with your natural eyes. Releasing things that could change your life, and you may not even realize it until later.

I believe some of those prayers are critical. Urgent. They may even be the difference between life and death.

I've experienced that firsthand.

Let me tell you a story.

DIVINE INTERVENTION

There was a time back in my corporate days when I was working as a marketing manager at one of the top insurance companies in the world. On this particular day, I was scheduled to make the drive from Los Angeles to Bakersfield, California, about two hours up the 5 freeway, to meet with one of our independent agents in the region.

It was business as usual. Until it wasn't.

As I was driving, something inside me shifted. I started to feel troubled. Not panicked. Not anxious. But uneasy. There was a weight in my spirit. An unsettling that I couldn't name. It didn't come with a clear warning or a mental explanation. It came as a feeling. Eerie. Tense. Almost ominous.

And even though my mind didn't know what was going on, my spirit did.

Out of nowhere, I opened my mouth and began to pray in my divine language. No script. No prompting. Just flow. Sounds, syllables, language I didn't understand poured out of me for what felt like forty-five seconds. And then, just as suddenly, it stopped.

Moments later I came upon a terrible car crash. It had *just* happened. There were no first responders. No flashing lights. Just metal, debris.

I had arrived seconds after the collision.

And suddenly it all made sense.

There's a verse in 1 Corinthians that explains what happened perfectly: "For if I pray in tongues, my spirit is praying, but I don't understand what I am saying" (1 Cor. 14:14 NLT). That's exactly what it felt like. My understanding was unclear, but my spirit was engaged. The Spirit of Knowing doesn't need a full download to act. It doesn't wait for confirmation or logic. It simply responds.

And when you aren't in a position to pray for what's coming—when danger hasn't been revealed—you are not left uncovered. "The Spirit Himself makes intercession for us with groanings which cannot be uttered" (Rom. 8:26). That's what happened that day. The Spirit knew what I didn't. The Spirit prayed when I couldn't. And I'm absolutely convinced: This was divine intervention.

He knows. Even when you don't. Even when danger hasn't yet shown up. Even when your understanding is unfruitful, unclear, or unavailable.

He knows.

THE FULLNESS OF DIVINE INTELLIGENCE

Divine language is amazing, no question. But it's only one of the many ways the Spirit expresses himself in our lives. Divine Intelligence is bigger than language. It's the Spirit working within us, reshaping how we think, how we lead, how we love, how we move.

It transforms our decisions. It enhances our creativity. It solves problems that logic can't untangle. It brings clarity to situations that feel impossibly complex.

This is not just spiritual. It's practical. It's not just about prayer. It's about power. To move with wisdom. To see through the surface. To respond from Knowing.

I've experienced it firsthand.

One of the greatest honors of my life was writing my second book, *Wholeness: Winning in Life from the Inside Out*. I poured my journey into that book—pain, healing, restoration, and insight I didn't even know I had. But here's the beautiful part: To this day, I've had dozens of licensed, trained, and highly educated therapists, psychologists, and psychiatrists tell me they use *Wholeness* with their clients.

They call it transformative. I call it Divine Intelligence. Because I know what I brought to that book. And I know what flowed through me that wasn't mine.

Paul writes in 1 Corinthians 12:8 that one of the manifestations of the Spirit is the word of knowledge—divine insight. A Knowing that goes beyond anything you could study or research. Something you didn't learn, but you know. Why? Because the Spirit wanted you to know it. Because someone needed it. Because the Spirit is always ready to move through those who are willing to listen.

This is a resource we must not take lightly.

Divine Intelligence is not optional for the life you've been called to live. It is vital. And it's not reserved for pastors or prophets or authors or scholars. It's for *you*.

All you have to do is ask.

And if you haven't yet received the Spirit—if you've never opened your heart to this gift, or maybe you're unsure whether you have—you can receive him today. Right now. There's no audition. No spiritual résumé. Just a willing heart and a simple ask.

The Spirit is not trying to hide. He's ready to reveal. To empower. To walk with you through life as your guide, your counselor, your inner wisdom, and your steady companion.

Let's take a moment right here. Let's pray this prayer together.

> *Holy Spirit, I welcome you into my heart, mind, and soul. Fill me with the fullness of your essence. Baptize me in all of who you are, that I might walk in the resource of Divine Intelligence, so that I can be everything you created me to be. In Jesus' name, amen.*

I cannot wait for what's going to unfold in your life.

You've begun something powerful. Something personal. Something eternal. And we're just getting started.

In the next chapter, I'm going to introduce you to something most people don't even know they have—an organ of perception.

This is the invisible faculty within you that connects directly to your first sense, your Knowing. It's how you sense truth before you can explain it. It's how the Spirit communicates beneath the noise. It's where intuition meets Divine Intelligence. And once it's awakened and aligned, it changes everything.

We're going to unpack what it is, how to recognize it, how to sharpen it, and how to flow in Knowing like never before.

Let's keep going. There's more waiting for you. More Knowing to come.

FIVE

DISCOVERING YOUR KNOWER

IN THE PREVIOUS CHAPTER WE EXPLORED THE POWER and presence of the Spirit—the source of Divine Intelligence, the one who leads us into truth, gives language to our mystery, and prays for us when we don't know what to say.

But now that the Spirit has been introduced, received, and welcomed, the question becomes this: How do I begin to hear, sense, and follow what the Spirit is revealing?

This is where many people get stuck. They've asked. They've received. But they still feel unsure. Not because the Spirit isn't speaking but because they haven't yet learned how to recognize the place where divine truth is perceived.

That place is what I call your "knower."

It's the internal sense that God has placed within you. The part of you that discerns what's real, what's true, and what's *him* even before your mind can explain it.

Your knower is not a guess. It's not a feeling. It's not even intuition. It's spiritual awareness. The first sense that was given to you by God. And once it's awakened, you begin to realize that you were never meant to figure life out. You were meant to Know.

Now, let me be clear: This doesn't mean we're called to be all-knowing. We're not becoming omniscient like God. But we *are* invited into a journey of increasing awareness, wisdom, and Divine Intelligence.

Paul says it this way: "Now I know in part, but then I shall know just as I also am known" (1 Cor. 13:12). We're growing. And the path of growth is illuminated with each step we take. "The path of the just is like the shining sun, that shines ever brighter unto the perfect day" (Prov. 4:18). Knowing is a journey. It unfolds over time. And every moment of clarity, every glimpse of truth, every whisper of direction is a sign that you are walking in the light, moving steadily toward the fullness of who you're becoming.

In this chapter we will explore what your knower is, how to recognize it, how to train it, and how to trust it. The more you learn to flow with your knower, the more clarity you'll carry in every part of your life.

This is the next step in your journey toward Knowing. Let's begin.

YOU WERE BUILT TO PERCEIVE

Back in chapter 2 we uncovered a foundational truth, that Knowing isn't just something we develop over time. It was our first sense.

Before we saw, heard, touched, or spoke, we knew. Not through reasoning. Not through mental processing. But through a spiritual awareness that God placed within us from the beginning. This leads us to an intriguing question: If Knowing was our first sense, wouldn't God have given us something to perceive with? Just like he gave us eyes for seeing, ears for hearing, hands for touching, a nose for smelling, and a tongue for tasting, wouldn't he have given us something to perceive spiritual truth with?

The answer is absolutely. And the Bible reveals it in a fascinating and often overlooked place.

In Hebrews 5:13–14, the writer is teaching about spiritual maturity—about how some remain infants in the faith while others grow into depth and discernment. And in that context the writer uses a powerful word: "But solid food belongs to those who are of full age, that is, those who by reason of use have their senses exercised to discern both good and evil" (5:14). That word *senses*, at first glance, sounds like it's referring to our physical faculties. But in the original Greek, it's a rare and extraordinary word: *aistheterion*. It's so rare, in fact, that it appears only once in the entire Bible. And its literal meaning? "Organ of perception."

This means that God, in his brilliance, didn't limit us to navigating spiritual reality with natural perception alone. He embedded within us an inner faculty designed to engage with divine truth. A spiritual receiver. A channel. A place within the soul where heaven speaks and awareness awakens.

The organ of perception is where wisdom lands. Where discernment begins. Where direction is confirmed. It's not driven by data, and it doesn't require explanation. It simply knows.

It's the space where the Spirit whispers and something inside you recognizes it before your thoughts catch up. It's not a hunch. It's not a guess. It's not a byproduct of emotion or instinct. It is a God-given capacity, woven into your design, so that you can walk with God not just by faith but by spiritual sensitivity.

And here's the beautiful truth: You already have it.

You don't have to create it. You don't have to chase it. You just have to tune in to it.

In the next section we'll uncover what it feels like, how to recognize it, and how to learn the language of your knower.

Because once you discover it, everything starts to become clear.

LEARNING TO RECOGNIZE YOUR KNOWER

Knowing has always been there.

You may not have called it that. You may have called it intuition. A gut feeling. A vibe. A hunch. Déjà vu. Some write it off as overthinking. Others dismiss it as coincidence. But that whisper, that nudge, that quiet sense that something's off or something's about to happen—that might've been your knower peeking its head above the surface asking to be seen.

The truth is, most of us don't need to discover our knower. We just need to recognize it.

It's not something new we're trying to get. It's something ancient that's been with us all along. The real journey is about becoming more aware of it, learning how to trust it, and cultivating the kind of environment where it can grow into maturity.

As I reflect on my own life, I realize I've had a knower for as long as I can remember. As a little boy, I could sense what to trust and what to walk away from. As a teenager growing up in the inner city, I learned to listen to that quiet sense of danger in the air. I'd leave the party early. Slip out of the mall. Not out of fear but out of Knowing. And sure enough, I'd find out later that a fight broke out. A shooting happened. Something went down that I had no reason to expect.

I've known what it's like to be in a relationship and feel the weight of something that isn't right before any evidence existed. Before a conversation, before a confession. And more often than not, the truth would eventually rise to meet what I already sensed: What I felt wasn't suspicion. It was Knowing.

Now, let me be clear—these are early signs. Elementary expressions. Surface-level examples of a much deeper reality. But like the first notes of a song, or the first brushstrokes on a canvas, they matter. Because they show us what's possible.

What we often call "a vibe" might actually be your knower asking for your attention. What we label coincidence might be a glimpse of what's happening in the unseen. And what we call instinct might be your spirit trying to speak in a language your soul hasn't yet learned to trust.

Your knower doesn't just want to protect you from being cheated on. It's not just about sensing bad energy in a room. Those moments matter, but they're the doorway, not the destination.

Knowing is meant to grow. To mature. To evolve into a trustworthy spiritual compass, able to discern truth in the big moments of calling, alignment, transition, and divine assignment.

But before it grows, it must be recognized. Before it can lead you, it must be heard. And the more you pay attention, the more it speaks. Not in sentences but in sensation. Not in volume but in clarity.

The knower doesn't shout. It nudges. It echoes. It waits to be honored.

And when you learn to recognize it, you begin to walk differently. Not in doubt but in discernment.

TRAINING THROUGH STILLNESS

Training your knower doesn't begin in action. It begins in awareness, and awareness starts with stillness.

One of the best biblical pictures of this comes from the life of an ancient and highly revered prophet named Elijah. At one point in his journey, Elijah spirals—mentally, emotionally, spiritually—just after one of the greatest mountaintop moments of his life. He has just called down fire from heaven and defeated nearly a thousand false prophets. It was a breathtaking demonstration of God's power.

But immediately after that, a voice comes. A threat from his nemesis named Jezebel. And suddenly Elijah—this bold, powerful prophet—is running for his life.

He ends up in a cave. Hiding. Afraid. Disconnected.

This moment is so important because it mirrors the very thing that can disrupt our Knowing: noise. The voice of fear. The weight of success. The exhaustion of doing too much. Sometimes life gets so loud that you can no longer hear the voice that led you to the mountain in the first place.

God speaks to Elijah in that cave, but not how Elijah expects.

First comes a violent wind. Then an earthquake. Then fire. But Scripture says God wasn't in any of those. Then comes a still, small voice. And that's where the shift happened. Stillness recentered Elijah's Knowing.

And the same is true for us. "Surely I have calmed and quieted my soul, like a weaned child with his mother" (Ps. 131:2). Stillness isn't weakness. It's not passivity. It's a strategy. Because when the soul quiets, the knower wakes up.

If you want to train your knower, you have to make space for it to speak. Not shout but whisper. Not demand but nudge.

HOW TO PRACTICE STILLNESS

Stillness isn't about silence on the outside. It's about surrender on the inside.

Here are a few ways to begin:

- Start with the breath. Close your eyes. Inhale slowly. Exhale slower. Let your body know it's safe to stop striving.
- Put away your phone. Even if just for five minutes. Make space for God to speak louder than your screen.
- Set a timer. One minute. Three minutes. Don't aim for forever—just long enough to remember that peace is always available.
- Speak nothing. Ask nothing. Simply be. Stillness isn't performance. It's presence.

- End with gratitude. Whisper "thank you"—not because everything is perfect but because you paused long enough to feel the presence that is.

Stillness is not passive. It's powerful. And the more you practice it, the more attuned you'll become to what's already within you. Once you are still enough, your knower—that divine organ of perception—will begin to speak more clearly, confidently, and consistently in your life.

TRAINING YOUR KNOWER

But stillness alone isn't enough. Once you begin to recognize your knower, you have to learn how to train it. And that training comes through one simple process: trial and error.

In Hebrews 5, the same verse where the writer speaks of the "organ of perception," it also says, "Solid food belongs to those who are of full age, that is, those who by reason of use have their senses exercised to discern both good and evil" (v. 14).

By reason of use.

That means you can't sharpen your knower by thinking about it. You sharpen it by using it. Just like a muscle, it grows through exercise. And that means acting on it. Testing it. Stretching it.

And yes—sometimes getting it wrong.

Your knower won't grow because you always get it right. It grows because you lean in, pay attention, and learn from the results.

One of the most powerful lessons in training your knower is when you sense something but ignore it, and pay the price.

I'll never forget a time when I was preparing to make a major investment. I did my research. Ran the numbers. Checked all the boxes. Everything on paper looked flawless. But something in my spirit didn't feel fully at peace. There was a subtle hesitation. Nothing dramatic, just a quiet pause. Still, I moved forward. I entered into contract and invested a significant amount of money. Not long after, it all fell apart.

It wasn't a full scam, but it was close. And although I was able to get out of the deal, it still cost me. I lost money. Time. Energy.

But don't feel sorry for me. Because what I lost in money, I gained in Knowing.

That experience didn't weaken my knower, it strengthened it. Now I listen differently. I trust the pause. I value the hesitation. I understand that the voice of Divine Intelligence doesn't need to shout. It just needs to be honored.

And I also understand this: Sometimes what looks perfect on paper isn't aligned with the Spirit. Scripture says, "Every good gift and every perfect gift is from above, and comes down from the Father of lights" (James 1:17). And, "The blessing of the LORD makes one rich, and He adds no sorrow with it" (Prov. 10:22).

So yes, I believe that what's "too good" might actually be just good enough for God to give you, but only when your knower says so.

Because discernment isn't about suspicion. It's about alignment.

And the only way to learn it is to live it.

TRUSTING WHAT YOU SENSE

There's hardly a greater feeling than knowing you've got what you've got. The kind of confidence that comes not from arrogance but from alignment.

Over the years, as I've continued to train, sharpen, and develop my organ of perception, I've learned to trust myself more. Not because I think I'm flawless but because I know I'm not operating blindly. I've trained my knower. I've paid attention to it. I've honored it. And now I walk with more confidence. I don't have all the answers, but I know how to recognize truth when it shows up.

I trust my life because I trust my ability to sense. And I trust what I sense only because I've developed it. I've worked on it. And it's grown with me. I've met people who check all the boxes. Everything on paper is great. They've got charisma, credentials, and charm. But something deep inside me signals, *Not yet. Walk slowly. Pay attention*. And although others might call it overthinking or being overly cautious, I call it wisdom.

Because I've learned that what I can't see in the present is often what someone might become in the future. And while God is full of grace, he's also full of insight. Sometimes he shows you the preview so you don't have to sit through the whole movie.

Recently I was reflecting on the difference between strength and power. And here's what I realized: Strength is what you've been given. Power is what you develop.

The organ of perception is a spiritual strength God has already placed within you. But power comes through discipline. Through use. Through resistance. Through consistent alignment with the Spirit of Knowing.

Power isn't just the presence of potential. It's potential put to work.

That's what trusting your knower looks like.

One of my favorite quotes from Kobe Bryant goes something like this: "I had talent, but I worked as if I had none." That's how I approach Divine Intelligence. I may have been given a spiritual gift, but I work it like it depends on me, because, in many ways, the development of it does.

It's the same thing I tell my kids: Anything you commit to practicing diligently, you will get good at. And when you know you've done the work—when you've prayed, when you've slowed down, when you've sat with God, when you've chosen integrity over impulse—you walk differently. Preparedness builds trust. Practice builds confidence. And confidence activates your Knowing.

So yes, trust your knower. Not recklessly. Not impulsively. But as someone who's been developing it. As someone who knows that this isn't guesswork. It's spiritual partnership.

When you believe that you have a God-given ability to perceive, when you trust that the Spirit is backing your discernment, and when you've been faithful to grow in it, you can trust what you sense.

Because trusting what you sense is how you step fully into the rhythm of Divine Intelligence. And that's where the real Knowing begins.

TUNING THE KNOWER

It's one thing to recognize your knower. It's another to sharpen it. But even after you've trained it, there's one more essential step: You have to tune it.

Just like a piano that's been played hard or a guitar that's sat too long between sessions. Even the most beautiful instrument can drift out of tune. And when that happens, the notes it plays may be heartfelt, but they won't be right.

The same is true with your organ of perception.

Your knower may be real, and even growing, but if it's not aligned—if it's not in harmony with truth—it can start playing the wrong melody.

Because there are other voices.

There's the voice of self—driven by desire, insecurity, or fear. There's the voice of the Enemy—subtle, accusatory, manipulative. And if we're not careful, those voices can start sounding like God's, especially when they echo what we *want* to hear.

That's why your knower must be tuned to truth. Truth is your tuning fork. It's how your knower stays aligned in a world that keeps shifting its pitch.

And not just truth as an idea. Truth as an anchor. Truth as a discipline. Truth as a commitment. Proverbs tells us, "Buy the truth, and do not sell it" (23:23). In a world filled with noise, filters, and half-truths, truth is not a commodity, it's an investment. And once you have it, you hold on to it. You don't trade it for comfort. You don't exchange it for popular opinion. You buy it and you never sell.

Paul writes in 2 Thessalonians, "[They perish] because they did not receive the love of the truth, that they might be saved" (2:10). This passage is about deception in the last days, and it reminds us that the only thing that will keep us from being deceived is the cultivation of a love for the truth. Not just an appreciation of it. Not just a respect for it. But a love for it.

Loving the truth means tuning your knower to it again and again, even when it's inconvenient. Even when it challenges your comfort zone. Even when it requires change.

So how do you tune your knower?

Yes, through stillness. Yes, through quiet. But also through Scripture. Through trusted spiritual community—people who live aligned, not just inspired. Through teachers and voices that don't just stir you but confirm what God is already saying. That's why I always say, "Don't come to church just to be taught. Come to be confirmed." Your knower might already be speaking. Sometimes you just need someone to help you recognize the sound.

So no, don't tune your knower to culture. Don't tune it to comfort. Don't even tune it to your feelings. You'll know you're tuned to culture when your convictions shift with the crowd. You're tuned to truth when peace remains even when it's unpopular.

Tune it to truth. Tune it to the Word. Tune it to alignment. And above all, cultivate a deep, unwavering love for the truth.

Because when your knower is in tune with truth, deception can't hold space. You won't be easily swayed. You'll move with clarity, confidence, and calm, because you'll know what you know.

And that's when your life begins to resonate. Not just with sound but with Spirit.

WHEN KNOWING BECOMES NAVIGATION

Something shifts when your knower moves from being something you sense in moments to something you live from.

That's when Knowing becomes more than a spark, it becomes a compass. A way of seeing. A way of choosing. A way of being. And when that happens, your life doesn't just feel spiritual, it becomes aligned.

You began this chapter by awakening to something that's always been there. An internal sense. A God-given ability to perceive what eyes can't see and ears can't hear.

From there you began to recognize it. Train it. Sharpen it. Tune it.

Now it's time to walk in it.

Knowing becomes navigation when it's no longer a last resort but a first instinct. When instead of reacting to life you begin responding to the Spirit. When you lead meetings, engage in relationships, make decisions not just with strategy but with Spirit-led sensitivity.

It looks like pausing before responding. Asking questions before assuming. Letting peace confirm a yes and letting pressure signal a pause.

It looks like sitting with God when everything feels clear, just to make sure. And it looks like trusting that nudge when you can't yet explain it to anyone else.

Knowing becomes navigation when you no longer doubt the stillness, because you've seen how many times that stillness saved you.

When you no longer second-guess your delay because you've learned that waiting is a form of wisdom.

When you no longer ignore the dissonance because you've tuned your knower to truth.

And when that becomes your rhythm, you don't just feel guided, you become a person of guidance.

So what does this look like in daily life?

It's the leader who trusts peace over pressure in decision-making. It's the parent who discerns what their child isn't saying out loud. It's the creative who senses when to pause and when to publish. It's the believer who no longer chases signs but walks in steady alignment with the Spirit.

You don't need to chase clarity anymore. You *carry* it.

Because when you've discovered your knower, trained it through stillness and practice, tuned it to the Word and to truth, you can begin to live from a place of wisdom that doesn't waver. A place where you move not with fear but with flow. Not with perfection but with peace. Not with performance but with presence. That's what navigation by Knowing looks like. And this is only the beginning.

Let's pray together.

God, I believe you have equipped me with an organ of perception—the ability to perceive your truth in any given moment.

Lord, instill in me an even greater hunger for truth. May I be surrendered to it. May I crave it. May I love it.

I thank you that as I desire truth, as I value this unique gift, as I sharpen it, trust it, and put it to practice, you will make me all the wiser in my Knowing.

All for your glory. In Jesus' name, amen.

Now that you've discovered your knower, trained it, and tuned it, you might think the next step is more knowledge. More revelation. More understanding.

But what if the next step is ignorance?

I know that may sound strange, but what if the very thing that deepens your Knowing is the awareness of what you don't yet know?

A prominent scientist once said that science isn't driven by knowledge, it's driven by ignorance. Because ignorance, when acknowledged with humility, creates hunger. And hunger leads to discovery.

The same is true in the realm of the Spirit.

In the next chapter we will explore what it means to embrace the catalyst of ignorance, and how admitting what we don't know can actually accelerate us into the next dimension of Knowing.

Let's continue the journey.

There's more waiting for you. More Knowing to come.

SIX

THE CATALYST OF IGNORANCE

IN THE PREVIOUS CHAPTER WE EXPLORED THE incredible gift God has given us—an internal organ of perception, a spiritual faculty designed to help us discern truth in real time.

We talked about recognizing it. Training it. Tuning it. And ultimately, learning to trust it.

But now we come to a new phase in the journey of Knowing. Because as much as we've been given, there's still one powerful force that often gets overlooked in the pursuit of wisdom: ignorance.

We often think of ignorance as something shameful—something to hide, deny, or correct as quickly as possible. In our information-saturated world, not knowing is often viewed as weakness. But what if ignorance, instead of being a dead end, is actually a door?

What if it is the spark that ignites discovery? What if it is the key to deeper Knowing?

In the world of science, this isn't just a theory, it's a principle. Neuroscientist Stuart Firestein, in his book *Ignorance: How It Drives Science*, makes a bold and liberating claim: "Ignorance is not something to be ashamed of, it's the engine that drives science." Science doesn't advance because it has all the answers. It advances because it keeps asking better questions. And those questions are born not from knowledge but from ignorance. That may sound like a contradiction, but it's not. It's a perspective shift. And it's one that aligns beautifully with the journey of divine Knowing.

Because here's the truth: The same principle that drives science forward is the one that deepens spiritual wisdom. Ignorance doesn't disqualify us from Knowing, it invites us into it.

God is not disheartened by our lack. Scripture shows us over and over again that humility and hunger—not certainty—are what unlock revelation: "The fear of the LORD is the beginning of wisdom" (Prov. 9:10). And, "He gives wisdom to the wise and knowledge to those who have understanding" (Dan. 2:21). The real danger is not ignorance itself. It's the refusal to acknowledge it. Because when we can admit what we don't know, we make space for something greater to be revealed.

This chapter is about reimagining ignorance not as a deficit but as a catalyst.

You're going to discover that:

- Ignorance is a starting point, not a flaw.
- Humility is the soil where revelation grows.
- Curiosity is spiritual hunger in disguise.
- Questions aren't obstacles, they're invitations.
- Divine Intelligence is most powerful when we admit we don't know everything.

We'll look at how science embraces uncertainty, how Scripture reveals successive layers of Knowing, and how the most powerful transformations often begin with a simple, honest prayer: "Lord, I don't know . . . but I want to."

This isn't just a chapter, it's a posture. One that turns not knowing into the very spark that draws us closer to the one who knows all.

Let's begin.

A NEW PERSPECTIVE ON IGNORANCE

We've already established that ignorance isn't the enemy of Knowing, it's the entry point. But what makes it powerful isn't just the absence of answers. It's the posture it produces. When embraced with humility, ignorance creates curiosity. It creates space. It opens a conversation with God that wouldn't happen if we thought we already knew everything.

As we've already discussed, ignorance is considered essential in the world of science. It's the questions, not the certainty, that pull us forward toward a truer kind of certainty. Ignorance in the right hands is productive. It's the open field where new ideas are planted. It's the spark that ignites curiosity. It's the doorway to deeper truth.

Now apply that same principle to your walk with God.

What if spiritual growth isn't about collecting more information but about having the humility to admit what you don't yet know? What if you're not stuck, you're just standing at the edge of a question that God is inviting you to ask?

Jesus didn't say, "Blessed are the certain." He said, "Blessed are the poor in spirit" (Matt. 5:3). Those who know they need more. Those who live with open hands, open hearts, and open questions. And when you can embrace that posture, ignorance becomes a gift. Not a wall but a window. Not an embarrassment but an entry point.

God isn't waiting for you to have all the answers. He's drawn to the one who says, "I'm listening. I'm open. I'm hungry to understand." That's why Scripture tells us, "If any of you lacks wisdom, let him ask of God, who gives to all liberally and without reproach" (James 1:5).

God loves honest ignorance.

He doesn't shame it. He responds to it. But only when it's paired with humility and hunger.

So let's shift the way we see it.

Ignorance isn't the absence of Knowing. It's the invitation to deeper Knowing. It's not the end of the journey. It's the spark that starts it.

EMBRACING THE GIFT OF NOT KNOWING

Take a moment to ask yourself:

- Where in my life have I been afraid to admit what I don't know?
- Have I been more focused on appearing certain than on being open?
- What question have I been standing at the edge of—one that might be a doorway into deeper truth?
- How would my posture shift if I saw ignorance not as a failure but as an invitation?

Now breathe this in: You don't have to know it all. You just have to be willing to ask, to seek, and to stay open. Because God is not repulsed by your questions, he's drawn to them.

THE POWER OF HUMILITY IN GROWTH

If ignorance is the catalyst, humility is the soil.

It's where revelation lands. It's where growth takes root. It's where Knowing becomes more than information. It becomes transformation.

Humility isn't about thinking less of yourself. It's about thinking accurately, recognizing that no matter how much you know, there's always more to learn. More to see. More to understand. More to be revealed. This is why humility is such a powerful position in the economy of God. It keeps us postured to receive.

James tells us, "God resists the proud, but gives grace to the humble" (James 4:6). Pride creates static. It interrupts the signal. It's hard to receive fresh insight when your posture says, "I've got this."

But humility turns the volume up on divine wisdom. It clears the interference so we can hear more clearly. It says, "God, I don't know everything, and I don't have to pretend I do. I trust you to show me what I need, when I need it."

That's how Knowing grows.

Because revelation is often timed, not just taught. God gives you what you're ready to receive, not always what you're eager to grasp. And humility keeps your heart ready. One of the greatest signs of spiritual maturity is the ability to say, "I didn't know, and I'm still learning."

Even Jesus, who walked in perfect alignment with God, grew in wisdom. Luke 2:52 tells us that he "grew in wisdom and stature, and in favor with God and man" (NIV). Let that sink in. Even Jesus had a process of growth. And if Jesus had room to grow in wisdom, how much more do we?

The most dangerous thing isn't being ignorant. It's being unaware of it. That's how pride traps you: It convinces you that what you know is enough. It shuts down curiosity. It closes the door to new revelation.

But humility flings that door wide open. It creates a space where the Spirit can speak. Where Divine Intelligence can enter. Where insight can be sown and truth can take root.

So if you want to grow in Knowing, don't chase the spotlight. Chase the quiet posture of a teachable heart. Because the more you humble yourself, the more God will trust you with what only the humble are ready to receive.

Let's pray this prayer together for a posture of humility.

God, I confess that I don't know everything, and I don't have to. I release the pressure to perform, and I surrender the pride that says I should have it all figured out. Teach me to walk with a humble heart. Make me teachable. Help me embrace the mystery and trust the process. I thank you that every time I lower myself, you lift me into higher wisdom. May I always stay in position to receive what you're ready to reveal. In Jesus' name, amen.

IGNITING THE HUNGER TO KNOW

If humility is the soil, hunger is the spark.

It's what turns curiosity into movement. It's what transforms openness into pursuit. And it's what draws us into deeper levels of Knowing.

Hunger is not a flaw. It's not a sign of lack. It's a sign of readiness.

In the world of science, discovery doesn't begin with answers. It begins with a question that refuses to go away. Researchers don't push forward because they know it all. They push because they know there's more to uncover.

It's the hunger for understanding that drives exploration. And that same hunger is essential for anyone seeking to grow in Divine Intelligence. "Blessed are those who hunger and thirst for righteousness, for they shall be filled" (Matt. 5:6). Hunger pulls on heaven. It tells God, *I'm not just curious, I'm ready. I don't just want to hear, I want to understand.*

One of the greatest shifts you can make in your spiritual life is to stop trying to feel "full" all the time and start learning how to feed your hunger. When you feel the ache for more, don't numb it. When you sense the tension of not knowing, don't silence it. Lean in to it.

Because that tension? That hunger? That divine unrest?

It's a sign that your next level of Knowing is calling.

And God responds to hunger.

He doesn't reward spiritual arrogance. He responds to spiritual appetite.

Hunger is what makes you ask. It's what keeps you knocking. It's what wakes you up in the morning wondering, *What does God want to show me today?*

Sometimes we want deeper revelation, but we've stopped asking real questions. We want to grow, but we're not leaning forward. We're hoping wisdom will interrupt us instead of pursuing it like treasure. But Proverbs tells us, "If you seek her as silver, and search for her as for hidden treasures; then you will understand the fear of the LORD, and find the knowledge of God" (Prov. 2:4–5). Wisdom doesn't hide from the hungry. Truth doesn't evade the seeker. Divine Intelligence flows where curiosity and courage meet.

So don't shrink back when you feel the hunger. Don't rush to fill the silence. Don't rush to resolve the mystery.

Let the hunger burn.

It's not there to frustrate you. It's there to form you.

And when you learn to steward hunger not as something to fix but as something to follow, you begin to walk in a Knowing that isn't forced. It's fed.

SUCCESSIVE DEGREES OF KNOWING

Knowing doesn't arrive all at once. It unfolds.

It comes in degrees. Layers. Revelations. Moments.

God rarely gives us the full picture at the start. Instead, he gives us just enough light for the step we're on, because the journey itself is part of the formation.

We want the whole blueprint. But God gives us building blocks. And it's not because he's withholding. It's because he's developing us.

This is what I call successive degrees of Knowing.

You receive one layer of revelation, and as you walk it out with integrity, obedience, and curiosity, God shows you the next. It's how trust is built. It's how spiritual stamina is developed. It's how our capacity for truth expands.

Jesus told his disciples, "I still have many things to say to you, but you cannot bear them now" (John 16:12). He wasn't holding back out of frustration. He was honoring the process. Some truths require preparation. Some revelations require stretching. Some levels of Knowing require you to grow before you can carry what's coming.

And I've lived this.

Over the past two decades one of the greatest areas of growth for me has been leadership. I've always been a natural leader. There was something intuitive in me that could gather, guide, and go forth. But I learned quickly that natural inclination isn't enough. Leadership must be developed. Skills have to be built. Wisdom must be layered over raw gifting.

There were times, especially early on, when I made decisions that in hindsight were immature. Not ill-intentioned, just underdeveloped. For a while I looked back on those decisions with regret. But now? I see them differently. God was developing me as a leader on a smaller level so I wouldn't make those same mistakes at a higher level. When more people, more weight, and more purpose were involved. The restraint was a gift. The delay was mercy. The process was the protection.

This same pattern has played out in countless other ways in my life. The more I know, the more I realize how much I don't know. And that realization doesn't disqualify me, it humbles me. It prepares me. It opens me to keep learning.

Knowing is not a moment. It's a rhythm. And when you embrace the process, you stop chasing instant clarity and start walking in steadfast revelation. The kind that leads to a deeper, truer certainty, even in an uncertain world. "To you it has been given to know the mysteries of the kingdom of God" (Luke 8:10). Not the *mystery,* the *mysteries.* Plural. Layered. Revealed in rhythm with your growth and God's timing. So don't be discouraged if you don't see it all yet. You're not behind. You're not missing anything. You're being formed.

And every degree of Knowing is preparing you for the next door. The next level. The next assignment.

And sometimes that preparation doesn't look like progress. Sometimes it looks like a pause. Let's pray this important prayer together right now.

God, thank you for being patient with me as I grow. Thank you for revealing truth in layers, for trusting me with wisdom as I'm ready to receive it.

Help me to be patient with the process. Help me not to despise the steps I haven't taken yet but to walk with faith, knowing that you are guiding me.

Teach me to forgive myself for what I didn't know then. To release the weight of regret for decisions I made from a place of inexperience or fear.

I let go of judgment toward the former versions of me, and I receive the grace, the compassion, and the love you have for who I am right now.

Make me sensitive to what you're revealing. Give me the strength to grow, the courage to ask, and the humility to keep learning.

I thank you that every step of the journey is drawing me closer to truth, to purpose, to you.

In Jesus' name, amen.

WHAT THIS BOOK TAUGHT ME ABOUT WAITING

We just prayed a prayer of release, one that confessed, "I don't know everything, and I don't have to." Looking back on my own journey, I realize how often God has used that very posture—not knowing—as a setup for something greater. One moment in particular stands out. It was a moment of preparation. And not the kind of preparation I recognized in real time. It's the story of this book.

What you're holding now—*Knowing*—didn't start this way. Originally it had a different name: *Called It*. The concept was sharp. I had energy, direction, ideas. I thought I was clear. I started writing, and the words came easily at first. But then came the interruptions. The slowdowns. The stretches when nothing I wrote felt right. I began to wonder whether I'd missed something.

Was this still the right message? Why had the clarity faded? Was I procrastinating, or was this a divine pause? At first I blamed myself. I figured I was being inconsistent, undisciplined, maybe even disobedient. I felt guilty. I tried to push through, but something in my spirit resisted. No matter how hard I tried to force the words, the inspiration wouldn't come.

Eventually it clicked. This wasn't failure, it was formation. I even spoke about it on my podcast, in an episode called "Positive Procrastination"—about how not all delays are detrimental. Sometimes the pause is protection. Sometimes what feels like procrastination is actually preservation, a sacred slowing down that guards what's growing from being born before its time.

That was me. God wasn't letting me move forward with *Called It* because I didn't need to publish something, I needed to birth something. And birthing takes time. The message I was trying to write hadn't fully formed in me yet. I had the structure, but not the substance. The framework, but not the fullness. I had good ideas, but not divine insight. What I didn't know then was that I didn't yet Know.

I couldn't yet see the depth, the language, the architecture—the spiritual blueprint of what this message was becoming. And I'm grateful I didn't force it. Because if I had written the book I originally envisioned, I would've missed the one I was meant to carry. *Called It* was the working title. But *Knowing* became the living truth.

It's easy to romanticize creativity as instantaneous and inspired. But some of the most sacred work takes time. It doesn't shout, it stews. It simmers. It settles in your spirit until it's strong enough to carry weight. This book wasn't written in urgency. It was written in reverence. It was born in waiting, in wondering, in wrestling. Even this had to unfold.

That's what this chapter is about. Sometimes the greatest breakthroughs don't come when we know everything, but they come when we're humble enough to admit, *I don't know yet, but I trust that if I wait, if I seek, if I stay open, I will.* That's not failure. That's formation. And more often than not, that formation begins with a question.

THE ROLE OF QUESTIONS IN SPIRITUAL DISCOVERY

Every degree of Knowing prepares you for the next. That's how we closed the previous section. And sometimes the key that unlocks that next level isn't another answer, it's the courage to ask the next question.

Questions are not the enemy of Knowing. They are the bridge to it.

In a world where confidence is often confused with the arrogance of having all the answers, it takes a different kind of strength to say, "I'm still learning. I'm still curious. I still have questions."

Questions are powerful, especially in the economy of God. They don't push you away from truth, they pull you deeper into it.

And Scripture is full of questioners.

- Abraham asked, "Lord GOD, how shall I know?" when God promised him the land of Canaan (Gen. 15:8).
- Moses asked, "Who am I that I should go to Pharoah?" when God called him to free his people (Ex. 3:11 NIV).
- David asked, "Why do You stand afar off, O LORD?" in the middle of deep frustration and pain (Ps. 10:1).
- Mary asked, "How can this be?" when the angel told her she would give birth to the Messiah (Luke 1:34).

Their questions weren't seen as weaknesses. They were the evidence of relationship. They asked because they were close. They asked because they trusted there was more.

And Jesus? He didn't rebuke their questions, he welcomed them. Even Jesus as a young boy was found in the temple asking questions of the religious leaders (Luke 2:46). And that posture didn't diminish his wisdom, it displayed it.

Earlier in this book we explored Jesus' teaching on asking: "Ask and it will be given to you; seek and you will find; knock and the door will be opened to you" (Matt. 7:7 NIV). He didn't say, "You'll get everything you want." He said, "If you ask, you'll receive." And what we receive, more often than not, is wisdom.

Sometimes we stop asking because we're afraid we'll get it wrong. But the real danger isn't asking. It's assuming we already know. Questions are not gaps in faith. They are evidence of hunger. They tell God: "I trust that there's more." "I believe you want to show me." "I'm still willing to grow."

So if you're in a season full of questions, don't see that as instability. See it as invitation.

Because asking is how we stay in rhythm with the Spirit. It's how we move from level to level in Divine Intelligence. It's how we find clarity. Not by having all the answers but by walking with the one who reveals truth in time.

This book is about walking the path to certainty in an uncertain world. But that kind of certainty isn't built by pretending we know everything. It's built by trusting the one who does.

So don't be afraid to ask. You're not being disloyal. You're being discipled.

Your questions aren't a detour. They're a divine invitation.

THE GLORY OF THE SEARCH

Throughout this chapter we've reimagined ignorance not as a flaw but as a force. We've seen that not knowing isn't a stop sign, it's a starting line. And when we approach it with humility and hunger, it becomes one of the most powerful catalysts for divine revelation.

Science has long understood this. Science doesn't progress because of what it knows, it progresses because of what it wants to know. It advances from a willingness to ask questions, challenge assumptions, and pursue answers that don't yet exist.

Faith is no different.

There's often been a perceived divide between faith and science, as if belief and inquiry are on opposite sides of the spectrum. But that's a false dichotomy. In truth, faith and science are companions on the same path, each reaching for something bigger than itself. Faith trusts that something is there. Science seeks to understand what that something is. And when both are postured in humility, they lead us into deeper Knowing.

Scripture affirms this beautifully: "It is the glory of God to conceal a matter, but the glory of kings is to search out a matter" (Prov. 25:2). The word translated *matter* in that verse literally means "a word, a revelation," a Knowing. This tells us something profound: God hides Knowing not to tease us but to transform us. To become the kind of person who searches with reverence. Who seeks with surrender. Who asks with expectation.

There is something royal, kingly, about the one who searches. In the tension between what God conceals and what we pursue, we're not just collecting facts, we're becoming more like him. Not because he is curious but because we're growing in Knowing, and that journey is what makes us more like him. So if you're still learning, if you're still hungry, if you're still asking, you're exactly where you're supposed to be.

Knowing isn't static. It unfolds. And part of that unfolding is remembering what's always been true: that before you ever searched for God, he already knew you.

That's where we're headed next.

In the next chapter we're going back to the beginning—to a truth so foundational, so identity shaping, that it has the power to reframe everything you've believed about your life, your calling, and your worth.

Because before you ever came to know God, you were already known by him.

SEVEN

FROM KNOWN TO KNOWING

Déjà vu, could you be the dream that I once knew?

—*Dionne Warwick, "Déjà Vu"*

HAVE YOU EVER HAD A MOMENT OF DÉJÀ VU?

You're in a place you've never been, standing in a conversation you've never had, yet somehow it feels familiar. It's not just a passing feeling. It's as if something inside you whispers, *You've been here before.*

The room. The sentence. The timing. You know you haven't lived it before, but it brushes against your awareness like a memory from a dream you can't quite reach.

Science has all kinds of theories for déjà vu—neural misfires, psychological echoes, time distortion. And maybe some of that is true.

But I've always wondered, What if there's more?

What if moments like that aren't just blips in the brain but reminders? What if they're brief encounters with something deeper, something eternal? A sense that your story didn't start the day you were born.

I'm not saying déjà vu is divine proof of anything. But I am saying this: If you've ever had that feeling that you were part of something before the beginning, you might not be wrong.

One day I stumbled across a passage of Scripture that shook me. A verse that didn't just speak to me, it read me. "Before I formed you in the womb I knew you, before you were born I set you apart"

(Jer. 1:5 NIV). Before I was formed, God knew me. Before I had breath, he had already set me apart. Before anyone else identified me, God had already assigned me.

That one verse changed how I saw my life. It gave me certainty in a world full of ambiguity. It gave me grounding in moments when I felt untethered. And it gave me the language to articulate something I had felt only as a quiet, intuitive truth: I was known.

And so were you.

This chapter is a return to that truth, a moment to realign with the divine reality that your life isn't random. You're not here by accident. And the path to knowing God begins by understanding this: He knew you first.

CRAFTED WITH INTENTION

There's something deeply healing about being told you're not an accident. That before you were formed—before your face had shape, before your lungs had breath—you were known. And more than that, you were intended. "Before I formed you in the womb I knew you, before you were born I set you apart." That verse has been read a thousand different ways by people in a thousand different seasons. But the first time it really read me, I knew I had stumbled onto something holy.

I first began to explore this truth years ago, when I wrote *Purpose Awakening*. I knew that purpose wasn't something you had to invent, it was something you were created with. But what I've come to see with even more clarity is this: Before there was ever a purpose to awaken to, there was a Knowing behind your existence.

You didn't begin the moment you were born. You began in the mind of God.

Your identity wasn't assembled after your arrival. It was spoken into being before your body ever took shape. That means your life is not random. Not your name. Not your personality. Not your voice, your wiring, your dreams, or your pace. You are the product of intentional design.

And when you see yourself that way—as known, chosen, and set apart—you begin to shed the labels that tried to name you after your pain, and you begin to return to the name God already knew.

It's hard to feel insecure when you know you were created on purpose. It's hard to compare yourself to others when you realize you were never meant to be a copy. It's hard to believe you're lost when you were known before you were formed.

This truth is not just comforting, it's foundational. Because when you know you were crafted with care, you stop living like someone trying to prove something and start living like someone with nothing to prove and everything to live for.

So before we move into purpose, before we talk about calling or assignment or legacy, let this truth settle deep into your soul: You were formed. But before that, you were known. And that Knowing changes everything.

Now, I want you to slow down for this part. I'm going to ask you two questions, and before you move on, I want you to pause. This is a good moment to grab your journal or open the notes app on your phone. Take a breath. And answer these questions with introspection and honesty.

- When you read the words "Before I formed you in the womb I knew you," what rises in your heart?
- Can you identify parts of yourself—your gifts, your voice, your perspective—that might reflect intentional design rather than random development?

FROM IDENTITY TO JOURNEY

You were not only known, you were positioned. Not just shaped but sent. Not just born but placed.

Your life is not a string of coincidences. It's a story unfolding in time, a path charted by the one who saw your beginning and your becoming at the same time.

So take heart. The journey ahead isn't random. It's already been seen. Already been measured. Already been prepared.

Let's go there next.

A JOURNEY ALREADY MAPPED

If your identity was crafted with intention, then your journey must have been as well. And the road you've walked—however winding, broken, or beautiful—has not caught God off guard.

Sometimes life feels like a series of random turns. A right decision here. A regret there. Doors that opened. Doors that slammed shut. Moments that felt like detours and others that felt like divine appointments.

We know how to celebrate divine appointments—those moments when the timing is perfect, the opportunity aligns, and you just know it was God. But there's another kind of moment that doesn't get celebrated as much: divine detours.

The job that didn't call you back. The door that didn't open. The mentorship that never materialized. The engagement that was broken off. The disappointment that looked like a setback but ended up being protection.

I've seen it in my own journey.

As a young minister, I longed for mentorship, not just from

anyone but from specific voices I held in high esteem. People I admired from a distance and hoped to one day sit under. I made the effort. I tried to get close. But for some reason it never happened. At the time, it felt like rejection. But now I realize it was a divine detour.

Had I been mentored by those individuals, I would've spent years learning things that didn't serve my voice, my calling, or my destiny. And worse, I would've had to unlearn those things later. And that, I've learned, is often harder than not learning them at all.

It wouldn't have been just a delay. It would've set me back. Because when you have to uproot something that was never meant to be planted, regrowth takes longer. God was doing me a favor I didn't have the perspective to appreciate.

And what I've come to understand over the years is this: You don't always get to choose where your blessing comes from. But God will always make sure you get what you need. And sometimes the greatest blessing is the one you thought you needed but didn't receive, because it would have ended up being a curse.

God doesn't just know who you are, he knows where you are. And more than that, he knows where you're headed. "Your eyes saw my unformed body; all the days ordained for me were written in your book before one of them came to be" (Ps. 139:16 NIV). The twists in your journey don't surprise him. They're part of the design. They are the training grounds of trust, the stretching places of perspective, the setup for the unfolding of deeper Knowing.

And just like you were formed with precision, you are also being guided with intention.

This doesn't mean everything you've experienced was God's doing. But it does mean nothing is beyond his redemptive reach. He knows how to bring you through every disappointment and detour and weave it into the fabric of your calling.

That job you didn't get. That relationship that didn't work out. That season that felt like delay or defeat. None of it disqualified you. In fact, it may have been preparing you so that when purpose called, you'd be ready to answer.

God is not just writing your story. He's already seen the ending. And the part you're in right now? It still fits.

So walk with confidence. Even when you can't see the whole map, trust that the one who drew it already knows where it leads.

YOU ARE ORDAINED

You weren't just formed with love. You weren't just placed with intention. You were born with purpose.

And not just a general, vague purpose but a personal, God-designed, tailor-made purpose that is already alive inside you. That's why Jeremiah 1:5 doesn't just say "I knew you" or "I set you apart." It also says, "I ordained you."

The word *ordain* means "to appoint, to designate, to assign." God was saying, "Before you ever got here, I already had something in mind for you to do."

But Jeremiah's response is where so many of us live. He didn't say, "Thank you, Lord. I receive that." He said, "I can't." "Alas, Sovereign LORD . . . I do not know how to speak; I am too young" (Jer. 1:6 NIV).

In other words, "You've got the wrong one."

And what does God say? "Do not say, 'I am too young.' You must go to everyone I send you to" (v. 7 NIV).

God doesn't argue, he redirects. He says, "Stop saying what I never said. Your words need to align with my Word."

And that's the tension so many of us face.

We sense purpose. We feel the call. But when the weight of it hits, when the opportunity arrives, when the door opens, we step back and say, "God, are you sure?"

I know that feeling.

There was a moment in my life when I was called into something bigger than I could imagine. God had led me—clearly, without a doubt—to step into the role of successor to the leader of one of the most globally impactful churches of our time. Not only that but to succeed a leader I respected deeply. Someone with spiritual authority, wisdom, and legacy.

There was no confusion about whether God had led me. Knowing had carried me there. But when I arrived—when I saw the scope of the assignment, the structure, the staff, the expectations—I was, if I'm being honest, overwhelmed.

It felt like too much. I began to question whether God had made a mistake. I thought, *Maybe this is for someone else. Someone stronger. Someone with more experience. Someone who looks more like what people expect.*

And then the light bulb went off: *You are ordained for this.*

I had to remind myself of what God already knew. That I wasn't stepping into this by accident. That I wasn't appointed by people, I was appointed by God. That this moment was already accounted for in my divine assignment.

And that same truth applies to you.

You were born with an assignment. You were born with a reason. You were born with something this world needs: a sound, a voice, a presence that no one else can bring.

That reminder changed everything.

I stepped into the assignment. I aligned my words and beliefs with what God had already said about me. And since that moment, things have gone incredibly well.

I have the respect of the people, both within the organization and beyond. But I never would've earned that respect until I first respected myself and, more important, respected the word God spoke over me.

Your purpose may not be global. It may not be platformed. But it is *yours*, and it is effective.

One person's impact doesn't outweigh another's in the eyes of God. What matters is alignment. What matters is obedience. What matters is that you say yes to what you've been appointed to do.

You don't have to figure it out. You don't have to fight for it. You don't have to chase it. You just have to receive it. And then walk in it.

So when you feel overwhelmed, when you feel like it's too much, when you wonder whether God got it wrong, remember: You are ordained.

Let's pray this prayer.

God, I thank you for ordaining me, for making me unique, distinct, and necessary. Thank you for channeling all of heaven's resources to support what you've called me to carry.

Give me the strength not to waver in my identity, calling, or purpose. And in the moments when I feel weak, in the moments when I feel overwhelmed, let me hear your voice again—that gentle, steady whisper reminding me: You are ordained.

Amen.

YOU WERE POSITIONED ON PURPOSE

If you were formed with intention, if your journey was mapped, if your purpose was ordained, then it only makes sense to believe this too: You were positioned on purpose.

Where you live. When you were born. The family you came

through. The city you're planted in. The circles you influence. Even the challenges you've had to navigate. None of it is wasted. None of it is random. It's all part of the assignment.

Sometimes we think if we had a different start, or came from a different background, we would've been farther along. But what if your start is part of your strength?

What if the very context that felt like limitation was the soil that God chose to plant you in because it would produce something in you that no other place could?

That's what divine positioning is about.

It means God didn't just ordain your life, he situated it. Strategically. Specifically. With influence and impact in mind.

You were born at the right time. Planted in the right place. Given access to the right people. Even the adversity you faced was factored in. And while it may not always feel that way—while some moments may seem like misplacement—God sees it all differently.

He knows what's in you. And he knows where your voice, your story, your gift, and your presence are needed most. "From one man he made all the nations, that they should inhabit the whole earth; and he marked out their appointed times in history and the boundaries of their lands" (Acts 17:26 NIV). You are not behind. You're not late. You're not out of position.

You are right where he needs you.

You may be like Esther, who didn't realize at first why she had been elevated. But eventually she came to understand that her life wasn't just about her, it was about timing. It was about purpose. It was about people who were connected to her obedience.

Esther was a Jewish girl who rose to become queen in a foreign land. She didn't get there by ambition, she was chosen. But when her people came under threat of annihilation, she hesitated. Speaking up for them meant risking her own life.

She thought about staying silent. She considered shrinking. She almost missed the moment.

But her cousin Mordecai said something that shifted everything: "Who knows whether you have come to the kingdom for such a time as this?" (Est. 4:14). And in that moment, Esther realized she had been positioned on purpose.

She was in the palace not for comfort but for courage. Not for personal gain but for the deliverance of others. Her position was the assignment.

The same could be said of you.

You are where you are for a reason. You are who you are for a reason. And if you keep saying yes—if you keep leaning in to what's been placed in your hands—you'll begin to see the fingerprints of God in places you once called coincidence.

You've been positioned on purpose. And that position is preparation for everything God is still unfolding in your life. This chapter has been a return to the origin story—not the moment you took your first breath but the moment God first thought of you. Before you were born, you were known. Before you were seen, you were set apart. Before you were aware of your own life, God had already written purpose into your DNA.

You are not random. You are not here by accident. You are not behind.

You were crafted with intention, placed with precision, ordained with purpose, and positioned with strategy. And when life feels heavy, when purpose feels bigger than your capacity, when you start to wonder whether God got it wrong, remember: He didn't just call you, he chose you. He didn't just assign you, he ordained you.

This is the foundation for your next step in the journey. Because divine Knowing doesn't just speak to where you are. It also speaks to where God is calling you to go.

In the next chapter we'll explore what happens when purpose requires movement—when Knowing leads you to the edge of a new place and obedience asks you to let go of the familiar. Because to fully walk in what God knows about you, you'll often have to be willing to leave what you've known about yourself.

Sometimes God will reposition you, not because you've done something wrong but because he's ready to take you somewhere greater. And when that moment comes, obedience becomes your greatest act of Knowing.

Let's keep going. There's more waiting for you. More Knowing to come.

EIGHT

THE MANDATE OF MIGRATION

> To step into the unknown with a God you trust is to leave what is safe for what is sacred.
>
> —*Bishop T. D. Jakes*

THERE COMES A MOMENT IN EVERY LIFE WHEN STAYING is no longer an option.

Not because what's behind you is bad but because what's ahead of you is bigger. Bigger than your current space can contain. Bigger than what your familiar surroundings can support. Bigger than the version of you that comfort has allowed to survive.

That moment is what I call the mandate of migration.

It's not just about relocation. It's about releasing what was so you can receive what is next.

It's about knowing when to leave a season, a mindset, a relationship, or an environment that once served your purpose or your calling but can no longer sustain the version of you that your future requires.

Because the familiar, while often safe, is not always sacred.

In fact, the greatest threat to your next step isn't failure. It's familiarity.

Familiar routines. Familiar fears. Familiar names, systems, and stories that keep you rooted in an identity you've already outgrown.

And if you're going to become all that God knows about you, you'll have to be willing to leave the places that know only who you've been.

One of the clearest pictures of this in Scripture is a man whose life was marked by movement. A man whose journey didn't just transform his own life but sparked a movement that is still unfolding to this day.

His name was Abram.

And before he became Abraham, the father of faith, he was a man called to leave everything familiar in response to a word from God. "The LORD had said to Abram, 'Go from your country, your people and your father's household to the land I will show you'" (Gen. 12:1 NIV). Abram didn't receive a destination, he received a departure. He didn't get a map, he got a mandate. And in that moment he became the embodiment of the migration mindset.

His journey of separation became the foundation of something far greater—a movement of faith, of promise, of purpose—that we're still part of today.

This is what happens when Knowing demands movement. When God says, "It's time to go."

And make no mistake, he still says it today.

THE CALL TO SEPARATE

Before God ever shows you the destination, he will usually test your willingness to leave.

That's how divine migration begins. Not with a detailed itinerary. But with a simple instruction: Go. Abram didn't receive coordinates. He received a command. "Go from your country, your people and your father's household to the land I will show you."

No explanation. No map. Just movement.

And embedded in that one word—"Go"—was the condition that would unlock his destiny: He had to be willing to leave the familiar.

God instructed Abram to leave three specific things:

- His country
- His family
- His father's house

Together, these three things form the framework of the familiar, as we'll see shortly. And yet God's first instruction was to leave them behind.

Why?

Because before God can reshape your identity, he has to remove you from the environment that shaped the old one. Purpose demands separation. Not because God is punishing you but because what he's preparing you for can't breathe in the space you're standing in. Sometimes God isn't calling you out of a location, he's calling you out of a limitation.

Because as long as you stay rooted in what shaped who you've been, you'll never fully step into who you're becoming.

And I've lived this firsthand.

When I first truly surrendered to God and began walking in purpose, I found myself drawn back to the church where I had embraced God for the first time at nine years old. It was a great church, full of integrity, strong leadership, and deep roots. My great-grandmother was one of the founding members. It had grown into a thriving community in Los Angeles, and when I returned, I was ready to give it everything.

And I did.

I served faithfully. I was there every time the doors were open. I was young, passionate, gifted, and on paper, it looked like I was the next generation of leadership for that ministry.

But then something unexpected happened.

God said, "Go."

Leave the environment. Leave the relationships. Leave the place where I was thriving. It was one of the hardest things I'd ever done. But I obeyed. And only later did I understand why.

As amazing as that church was, its vision, while powerful, wasn't big enough to contain what God had called me to do. It wasn't bad. But it was too small for the assignment I was born to carry.

God had called me to the world. To diverse people. To cities and systems. To voices I hadn't met and platforms I hadn't imagined. And to reach those people, I would need new perspective and, more important, new language.

Language that didn't yet live in the place I had come from. Language that would emerge only through obedience and migration.

And had I stayed, I never would have become what God knew about me before I was born.

So when God says, "Go," it's not rejection, it's redirection.

It's not about abandoning your past. It's about stepping into a future where he can show you what he sees in you.

This is the call to separate. As it was for Abram, so it is for us—it's where the movement begins.

WHEN COMFORT BECOMES A CAGE

Comfort is a beautiful thing—until it starts working against your future.

It's not always obvious. It's not loud or aggressive. It's subtle. Comfort whispers, *Stay a little longer. It's not the right time to move. You're doing fine here.*

But eventually comfort doesn't just feel good. It starts to feel necessary.

And that's when it becomes a cage.

A cage that keeps you in environments you've outgrown. A cage that convinces you the familiar is safer than the future. A cage that looks like peace but feels like pause.

Here's the truth: Most people don't miss purpose because they aren't gifted. They miss it because they aren't willing to leave what is comfortable. The longer you stay somewhere you've outgrown, the harder it becomes to imagine life beyond it. Comfort has a way of numbing your instincts, of silencing your knower, of softening your urgency to move. And the trap is this: Familiar doesn't fight you. It affirms you. It keeps feeding you just enough to feel productive, while slowly disconnecting you from the pull of where you're really supposed to be.

But you weren't built to settle. And when God is calling you to more, settling becomes dangerous. I've seen people miss divine appointments because they were too attached to a life they once prayed for. What was once a blessing now requires obedience to leave.

Because growth requires movement. And movement requires courage. There comes a time when staying is no longer being faithful, it's being afraid. And God, in his love, will start to make what was once comfortable feel cramped. He'll let the ground under your feet feel unstable. He'll pull back the sense of ease, not to punish you but to push you. Because he knows that if he doesn't disrupt your comfort, you might never discover what you're truly capable of becoming.

So if things have been shaking, if the ground under your feet has started to feel unstable, if the space that once felt like home now feels like a holding pattern, don't panic. You're not falling apart. You're being released.

What you're feeling might not be failure. It might be permission to move. Because when comfort becomes a cage, God will break it open so you can fly.

DIVINE DETOURS AND FORCED EXITS

Not every migration starts with a choice.

Sometimes it starts with a closed door. A contract not renewed. A friendship that falls apart. A career path that ends without warning. A why that never gets answered—or answered much later.

Divine detours and forced exits don't always look like God's work. In the moment, they look like disappointment. They feel like failure. They sound like silence. But often what feels like life falling apart is actually God pulling you out of what no longer serves your future.

I've experienced this firsthand.

Early in my professional career I was working what I believed to be my dream job. It was with a large national corporation, one I had planned to grow old in. There was upward mobility, strong benefits, and the kind of structure that made sense for where I was in life. The paycheck met my needs, and to be honest, I was good. Settled. Secure.

Until, without warning, I was fired.

No wrongdoing. No explanation that made sense. Just a termination I didn't see coming.

I was devastated. Not just because of the loss of income or routine but because my plans had been shattered and I didn't understand why.

But here's what I didn't know at the time: God was behind it.

What felt like a firing was actually a freeing. Because if I had stayed where I was, I would've missed everything that came next.

In just a few months I found myself in a new career. More money. A shorter commute. Greater clarity. Momentum. Favor.

And the best part?

Nearly a year later the same company that let me go admitted they made a mistake. They offered me my job back—with retroactive pay. So I pulled up in my new car, received the check I was due, and let them know, "You can't afford me anymore."

It was one of the most satisfying moments of my life.

But more important, it was proof.

Proof that God sometimes has to push you out of what you won't leave on your own. Proof that purpose doesn't always look like a promotion, it might look like a closed door. Proof that the end of what you planned can be the beginning of what he's ordained. "In their hearts humans plan their course, but the LORD establishes their steps" (Prov. 16:9 NIV).

Some of the greatest upgrades in your life will look like rejection on the front end. But if you trust the process, if you keep walking, if you keep listening, you'll realize it was never about what was taken from you. It was about what God was trying to give you next.

Don't curse the detour. Don't resist the exit. God might be saving you years of delay and launching you into a future you didn't know how to ask for. Because even when the migration is forced, the purpose is still divine.

Before you move on, take a moment to sit with what you've just read. We don't always recognize divine detours when they happen. Sometimes they show up as heartbreak, disappointment, or unexpected change. But buried in what feels like loss might be the very thing that launches you toward purpose.

These questions aren't here to stir up pain. They're here to reveal perspective. They're here to help you see where God's hand may have been moving even when his voice felt quiet.

Take a breath. Be honest. And invite the Spirit to walk with you through the next few moments of reflection.

For Reflection

- Can you recall a moment in your life when something ended unexpectedly? What did it feel like at the time?
- Looking back, is there any part of that experience that might have been God's redirection, even if you didn't see it then?
- Have you ever stayed in a place—professionally, relationally, emotionally—longer than you should have, simply because it was familiar?
- What might God have been trying to open up to you by closing the door you were holding on to?
- How might you respond differently now to a closed door knowing what you know about divine detours?
- Let your pen bear witness to the truth that's unfolding in you. Jot it down, honor it, and, when your spirit feels ready, move forward.

THE SHIFT BEFORE THE SHAPING

There is a moment after the breaking when the rebuilding begins.

It's quiet. But it's holy.

Because now that you've let go of what was, God can start revealing what's still holding on.

You've left the room, but has the room left you?

Have the words that shaped your identity, the systems that formed your perspective, the expectations you never chose been fully surrendered?

If you want to become all that God knows about you, you'll have to take inventory of what's still shaping how you see yourself.

Let's go there next.

WHAT'S SHAPING YOU?

Before you can fully walk in what God knows about you, you have to ask yourself, What shaped the version of me I've been walking in?

Because, just like Abram, many of us have been formed by familiar systems—systems that may have taught us how to survive but can't teach us how to become. That's why God didn't just tell Abram to go. He told him to leave behind three specific things: "Get out of your country, from your family and from your father's house" (Gen. 12:1). These weren't just directions. They were diagnostics.

Each one represents something deeper than geography. Each one speaks to the systems that shape what we believe about who we are and what we think we're allowed to become.

1. *Your country is representative of your environment*—your cultural context, your upbringing, your daily norms. It shaped what you called "normal." And if you're not careful, it will shape what you believe is possible.
2. *Your family is representative of relationships*—not just relatives but the voices that have influenced you the most. They shaped what you think is valuable, acceptable, expected.
3. *Your father's house is representative of identity inheritance*—what you were told about who you are. The assumptions. The labels. The expectations you never agreed to but learned to live under.

The hard truth is that much of what we think we know about ourselves was shaped by those systems, not by God. So before God can reintroduce you to who you really are, he often begins by disrupting the systems that falsely defined you.

This is why Knowing doesn't begin with answers. It begins with unlearning.

Because you can't fully embrace divine Knowing if your self-awareness is still tethered to systems that saw only part of you.

Let that settle.

You may have learned loyalty in your father's house, but you also learned limits.

You may have learned resilience in your environment, but you also learned how to shrink to stay accepted.

You may have found safety in familiar relationships, but you also learned how to mute your difference to stay included.

God doesn't dishonor where you've come from, but he will call you beyond it.

Because what he knows about you is bigger than what they named you. More complete than what your culture reinforced. More powerful than what your environment prepared you for. This is where Knowing gets real. Because real Knowing doesn't just tell you where you're going, it shows you what's still shaping how you see yourself. And when that happens, you'll start to understand: Leaving the familiar isn't just about geography. It's about identity. And until you're shaped by truth, you'll continue to walk in patterns built on survival, not purpose.

And survival has a voice. It teaches you to shrink, to doubt, to mistrust what's good. It forms beliefs that feel true, because they kept you safe, but they were never meant to shape who you are. We'll explore this more deeply in the next chapter: how trauma creates Misknowing and how unhealed experiences can secretly distort what we believe about ourselves, others, and even God.

But for now it's enough to acknowledge this: Some of what you know might not be truth. It might just be what helped you survive.

And God is inviting you into a Knowing that's shaped no longer by fear but by freedom.

THE COURAGE TO MOVE AND THE GRACE TO HEAL

You've now seen what separation requires. You've been reminded that obedience isn't just about going somewhere new, it's about becoming someone God already knew you were meant to be.

You've learned to name the systems that shaped you. To recognize when comfort is no longer safe. To honor divine detours even when they don't make sense in the moment.

But before this chapter ends, there's one more truth we need to sit with: Sometimes what holds us back isn't just external. It's not just the familiar routines, the old environments, or the people we've outgrown. Sometimes what holds us back is what trauma taught us to believe. Beliefs that were formed in survival. Assumptions that were shaped in pain. Lies that felt like truth because they kept us safe. And if we're going to fully embrace the Knowing that comes with movement, we'll also have to confront the Misknowing that trauma may have left behind.

That's where we're going next.

Because while obedience will position you, healing will free you. And to step fully into who God knows you to be, you may have to unlearn who pain tried to make you.

Sometimes the hardest thing to leave behind is the version of you shaped by what tried to break you.

NINE

MISKNOWING

TRAUMA'S SECRET SYMPTOM

> Trauma results in a fundamental reorganization of the way mind and brain manage perceptions. It changes not only how we think and what we think about, but also our very capacity to think.
>
> —*Bessel van der Kolk, The Body Keeps the Score*

WE OFTEN THINK OF TRAUMA AS AN EVENT WE SURVIVE. But trauma is not just what happened. It's also what we came to believe because of what happened.

It leaves behind more than memories. It leaves behind misbeliefs. Distorted truths. Survival-based "certainties" that feel like wisdom but are really wounds wearing a disguise.

This chapter is about a concept I call Misknowing.

Misknowing is what happens when your Knowing has been shaped by pain. When your perception has been formed not by truth but by trauma.

It's subtle. It's deceptive. And most of the time, it hides in internalized constructs that we call "facts":

- "I can't trust anyone."
- "I'm not safe."
- "People always leave."
- "I'm too much."
- "I'm not enough."
- "This is just how life is."

But what if those aren't facts at all? What if they're just defenses we've mistaken for discernment? What if the very beliefs we've leaned on to survive are now the same ones keeping us from becoming?

This is where the path to Knowing gets personal. To step fully into truth, we have to be willing to confront the Misknowing we picked up in the dark.

Not to shame ourselves but to set ourselves free.

This is where we begin.

WHEN KNOWING BREAKS DOWN

There's a kind of Knowing that doesn't come from truth. It comes from pain. From survival. From moments we never asked for but were forced to live through. Moments that didn't just leave memories, they left certainties. "I'll never be safe." "I can't trust people." "I'm not enough." "I always have to prove myself."

They feel like facts. But they're not.

They're trauma disguised as truth. And unless we confront them, we will keep living by them, shaping our decisions, our relationships, and our sense of identity by Misknowing.

Misknowing is what happens when trauma teaches you something about yourself, others, or the world that isn't true but feels true. It's what happens when pain becomes your teacher. When wounds become your filter. When you adopt certainties based not on revelation but on protection. And most of the time you don't even know it's happening. You're just trying to live. Trying to stay safe. Trying to hold it together.

So you build a life on "truths" that weren't meant to carry you.

You start navigating the world with instincts that kept you alive in the past but now keep you stuck in patterns that no longer serve who you're becoming.

This is when Knowing breaks down.

Not because you're broken but because something hurt you deeply and your soul made an agreement to survive that moment the only way it knew how. But here's the thing about survival: It gives you tools to get through trauma, but if you're not careful, you'll start building your identity with the same tools you were meant only to escape with.

Misknowing isn't weakness. It's evidence that something happened that your heart tried to protect you from. But now God wants to show you a new way of seeing. Not through shame. Not through self-blame. But through a process of reclaiming the truth beneath the lie.

This chapter isn't about digging up pain just to relive it. It's about naming what shaped you so you can finally release what's not true and walk in what is.

Because to truly know who you are, you'll have to unlearn what pain tried to teach you.

WHAT TRAUMA TEACHES YOU TO BELIEVE

Trauma doesn't just hurt. It teaches.

It teaches you who to trust. What to expect. What to fear. What to hide. What to perform. What never to forget.

But what it teaches isn't always truth. It's often just a version of reality shaped by pain.

And because trauma rarely gives you time to pause and process, you don't realize you're learning, you just start living by what you absorbed in order to survive.

I know this all too well.

I grew up in inner-city Los Angeles, where crime, drugs, prostitution, and police brutality weren't just news stories, they were part of the atmosphere. That kind of environment teaches you things. It teaches you how to read a room without looking at anyone. It teaches you how to carry fear on the inside and never let it show. And it taught me that the world was a dangerous place, so I needed to always be alert.

I was afraid, but I didn't know how to admit that. I just thought I was aware. I didn't cry. I couldn't. Fear was in the air I breathed, and that fear turned into hypervigilance. And here's the thing: That hypervigilance served me for a season. It kept me sharp. It kept me safe. But it also kept me stuck.

Later in life I read the book *The Gift of Fear* by my friend Gavin de Becker. He makes a compelling case that fear sharpens your instincts, that it can actually protect you. And he's right. But what happens when fear doesn't turn off?

What happens when the gift of fear becomes a lifelong subscription to anxiety? What happens when fear stops being a shield and starts becoming your lens?

I didn't fully understand the weight I was still carrying until I became a husband and father. My wife, Sarah, and I began noticing patterns in my parenting—hyperawareness, excessive caution, nervousness about our kids' safety.

We live in a gated community. There are cameras, guards, and layers of protection. And yet I'd say things like, "Make sure no one follows you home," "Double lock the door," "Always look over your shoulder."

Reasonable if you live in chaos. But that wasn't my children's world. It was my former world.

And then came a moment that, in hindsight, is absolutely laughable.

We were preparing to go out of the country as a family, and my daughter Makenzie, who was a freshman in high school at the time, mentioned to one of her girlfriends that we'd be out of town. Almost without thinking, I told her, "You shouldn't be telling your friends that! If they know we're going to be gone, they might see it as an opportunity to rob us."

I was dead serious.

It wasn't until Sarah gently brought it up later that I realized how ridiculous that sounded. She said, "So let me get this straight. You think a fourteen-year-old schoolgirl in ponytails is going to scale our fence, dodge the cameras, and rob us blind?"

We both laughed—because, honestly, it was ridiculous. But that's how trauma works. It trains you to see danger even where there is none. It doesn't ask whether the fear makes sense. It just whispers, *Be ready. Be careful. Stay alert. Always.*

Then came the moment I'll never forget. My nine-year-old, who had known only peace, privilege, and protection, started saying over and over again: "I'm scared."

That was it. That was the alarm bell. That was the moment I realized I had been importing my fear into their freedom.

And that fear wasn't wisdom. It was Misknowing.

It was a belief system I had formed in the fire of my past, but one that had no business shaping the world of my present. It kept me alert, yes. But it also kept me from resting. From trusting. From experiencing the peace of the season I had prayed for.

That's what trauma does. It gives you truths that don't apply anymore, but you still live by them. And unless you recognize them for what they are, you'll start raising your kids—or leading your team, or managing your life—not by revelation but by reflex.

Survival isn't bad. But it's not the same as Knowing.

Knowing is built on trust. Misknowing is built on tension. And until you confront it, you'll confuse the two.

WHAT HAS FEAR TAUGHT YOU TO BELIEVE?

Take a moment before you move on.

You may not have grown up in an environment like mine. But we all have places, people, or seasons that taught us how to protect ourselves. Taught us what to watch for. Taught us how to adapt.

But not everything that helped you survive was meant to help you live.

So before you go deeper, take a breath and ask yourself these questions—honestly, gently, without judgment.

For Reflection

- What environment or season of your life do you think shaped the way you see safety?
- Are there precautions you take that might actually be fear in disguise?
- Have you ever passed your fear onto someone else, intentionally or unintentionally?
- What belief about the world, yourself, or others feels true but may have been shaped by something you never had a chance to question?

Take a moment to capture your reflections, honoring the fresh perspective being revealed. When you're ready, feel free to continue.

MY STORY: DRIVE-BYS AND DADDY WOUNDS

Some wounds don't show up right away. They go underground. They hide in the places you don't talk about and sometimes don't even remember.

Not because they didn't happen but because what they told you about yourself felt too painful to examine.

That's how trauma works. It buries the moment, but it keeps the message.

Misknowing is born when the message of trauma goes unchallenged. And that message becomes a script. A lens. A certainty.

One of the most defining moments of my life was one I forgot for years. When I was sixteen, I was the victim of a drive-by shooting. I was driving home from a fast-food restaurant in inner-city Los Angeles when a car pulled up beside mine. A brief exchange. A flash of silence. And then gunfire.

A bullet entered my body near my right shoulder blade, ricocheted, and lodged in my throat.

By God's grace I survived. But something in me shut down.

Years later I went to the hospital for an unrelated reason—a routine appointment, an X-ray. After the first X-ray was taken, the technician clearly saw shrapnel across my right shoulder blade. The technician asked whether I had ever had an injury to my shoulder.

Without hesitation, I said, "No."

It wasn't a lie. I wasn't hiding anything. I genuinely didn't remember.

Sarah was with me. She looked at me, almost stunned. "You were shot in that shoulder," she reminded me.

And suddenly, like a fog lifting, it all came rushing back.

That's the thing about trauma. Sometimes you don't bury the event because you're ashamed, you bury it because your mind didn't feel safe enough to hold it.

That's Misknowing too.

Not just believing the wrong things but not remembering the real things. When trauma rearranges your perception, it doesn't just distort the truth, sometimes it buries it altogether.

I gave a quick, defensive answer: "Oh, yeah, I got shot when I was sixteen."

But the moment he asked, something in me began to shift. That familiar feeling crept in. Shame. Self-consciousness. The need to explain. To prove I didn't deserve it. And under that feeling was an assumption I didn't know I had. It said, *You're less valuable. You're tainted. People will assume the worst. This is your fault. You're not safe.*

That moment exposed a Misknowing I had carried silently for years. Even though I had built a life of purpose and prosperity, even though I was thriving on the outside, on the inside something still believed that moment defined me.

And then came the realization that changed everything: I hadn't buried the trauma. I had buried the lie trauma told me. It wasn't the shooting itself that marked me the most. It was the look in the eyes of the men who shot me—cold, detached, unbothered.

I didn't feel attacked. I felt discarded.

I felt like my life had no weight to them, like I was irrelevant. And that message—the message of worthlessness—lodged in my spirit just like that bullet had lodged in my throat.

But trauma isn't the end of the story. Because just like that bullet was discovered and seen, so was the belief that had been hiding inside me.

And God began to rewrite the message.

He showed me that getting shot wasn't shameful, it was a symptom of someone else's brokenness. That violence didn't define my value, it reflected theirs. That what had tried to devalue me was actually proof of the calling that made hell nervous.

And just when I thought the healing had reached its depth, God brought up another wound. A quieter one. But just as impactful.

My father.

We never had a close relationship. He was present, but distant. Strict. Hard. Demanding. I remember one time as a kid I spilled milk while pouring a bowl of cereal, and his response was so sharp, so angry, so out of proportion that something in me began to shrink. To hide. To question my worth. I learned to walk on eggshells. To overperform. To do things right so I wouldn't be criticized. But the truth is, nothing was ever quite good enough.

Even as I grew older and became successful, his criticism still found its way into conversations. And I thought I was okay. I really did. Until the day I tried to plan a Father's Day fishing trip to honor him, a simple gesture of love. He initially accepted. Then backed out last minute with critique and blame.

It hit me harder than I expected. And I realized this wasn't about the fishing trip. This was about a lifetime of trying to be enough for a man whose approval I never really felt. And when I finally broke down, weeping in the shower the Sunday before Father's Day, it wasn't just about the rejection of the gesture. It was a thirty-year-old cry rising up from the boy who had never been allowed to feel.

That cry cracked something open. And that's when the healing began.

Misknowing loses its grip when we stop trying to be okay and finally allow ourselves to feel what's real. It wasn't the bullet that almost broke me, it was the belief. It wasn't my father's words that held the most power, it was the meaning I gave them in silence. But now that meaning has been redefined. And what once shaped me in survival is being reshaped by truth.

NAMING WHAT YOU BURIED

You may not have been shot. You may not have had a strained relationship with your father.

But we've all been hit by something. And we've all been shaped by what we didn't feel safe enough to process. Sometimes the wound doesn't leave a scar on your skin, it leaves a belief in your soul. A belief that tells you who you are, what you're worth, or what you'll never be.

But what if those beliefs aren't true?

Take a moment here. Let the Spirit guide you back, gently, honestly, so you can begin to name what might have gone unnamed for too long.

For Reflection

- Is there a moment in your life that you've minimized but now realize may have shaped how you see yourself?
- What "certainties" did pain or rejection teach you that may not actually be true?
- Have you ever buried a wound so deep that you forgot it was even there until something triggered it years later?
- What survival instinct are you still living by that may have served you once but is now keeping you from peace?

- Is there a younger version of you who never got to feel the weight of what you went through? What would it look like to give that version permission to speak?

Before moving on, give yourself space to reflect and record what's emerging. Honoring these insights now will deepen what comes next.

IDENTIFYING YOUR MISKNOWING

Misknowing doesn't always announce itself. It doesn't come with flashing lights or bold declarations.

Most of the time, it hides in phrases like these:

- "That's just how I am."
- "This is just how life works."
- "People like me don't get that kind of opportunity."
- "I can't trust anyone."
- "I'm fine."

But beneath those statements there's often a belief that was inherited from pain. And that's what makes Misknowing so deceptive. It feels like wisdom. It sounds like discernment. But it's really fear in disguise.

Maybe you believe you're not enough not because it's true but because someone close to you always made you feel like you were too much.

Maybe you don't trust easily not because people are untrustworthy but because your heart learned early that love comes with a price.

Maybe you've overachieved, overworked, overproved your value not because you're driven but because some buried part of you believes you're still earning the right to be seen.

That's Misknowing. And the only way to break free from it is to learn how to spot it.

So here's a simple question that might reveal more than you expect: Where in your life are you reacting instead of responding?

Where are you controlling instead of trusting? Where are you withholding instead of receiving? Where are you self-protecting when you're no longer in danger?

Let's go deeper. Here are some signs that Misknowing may be at work:

- You push away compliments or affirmation because something inside tells you they aren't real or you don't deserve them.
- You say you're not afraid of love but you've built your entire dating life around avoiding vulnerability.
- You stay in relationships or jobs that drain you because you've internalized the belief that sacrifice equals value.
- You feel guilty when you succeed because you've learned to associate success with selfishness.
- You shut down emotionally in conflict not because you're cold but because you've equated emotional expression with danger.
- You equate being needed with being loved, so you constantly overextend yourself to earn connection.
- You fear rest because, somewhere along the way, rest started to feel like laziness, and achievement became your identity.

These reactions aren't flaws. They're clues. Signals pointing you to a deeper narrative that needs to be rewritten.

Here's another question to sit with: What "truth" have you never questioned because it kept you safe? Those are often the hardest to see. Because when a lie keeps you from being hurt again, it doesn't feel like a lie. It feels like Knowing.

But what if that Knowing has been keeping you small? What if that truth has been holding your purpose hostage? What if it's time to confront the belief not with judgment but with gentle, Spirit-led truth?

God's not asking you to fix everything in this moment. But he *is* inviting you to tell the truth about what you believe and where that belief came from.

You can't heal what you won't name. And you can't know what you haven't confronted.

This is where the transformation begins.

WHEN LOSS TEACHES YOU TO LEAVE FIRST

Before we talk about how to break the agreement with Misknowing, let me tell you one more story, because it exposed a pattern I didn't even realize I was living in.

I've experienced a lot of loss in my life. Some of it was expected. Much of it wasn't.

Growing up in the inner city, loss was a familiar sound. A background noise that never quite went silent. When I was eleven years old, I lost my best friend. Her name was Erica. She had moved into our neighborhood from the suburbs. She was kind. Sweet. Bright. But she got caught up in the wrong crowd. One day I got the news that she had been shot. Whether it was an accident or intentional, I never fully knew. What I did know was this: She was gone. And I was devastated.

But Erica wouldn't be the last.

Not long after, a young man from our neighborhood named Dwight was killed. Another good person in the wrong place at the wrong time.

Then in college, I got a call that one of my closest friends, Paul Pichon, had died in a car accident while driving cross-country to college in Atlanta. We had been best friends since middle school. Great guy. Great family. Bright future.

Gone.

And years later I lost my cousin Theo, a man who was more like a brother to me. He died suddenly in a motorcycle accident. No warning. No time to prepare. Just gone.

These losses, stacked over time, began to do something inside me. I didn't realize it, but the trauma was building a quiet mistrust not just of other people but of life itself. I became afraid to fully love, because somewhere deep down I feared that anything I loved could be taken from me.

So I started to withdraw. Not in dramatic ways but in subtle ones.

If someone got sick, I pulled back. If I sensed the end of something, I tried to get ahead of it by exiting emotionally first. Not to be cruel but to protect myself. And I thought I was fine—until the moment everything surfaced.

My grandmother had been sick. In and out of the hospital. I hadn't seen her in weeks. Not because I didn't love her but because I didn't want to feel what I feared was coming. Eventually I flew into Los Angeles from Dallas to visit her. When I arrived at the hospital, I planned to be strong. To encourage my aunt. To hold it together.

But when she asked me how I was doing, I opened my mouth

to speak, and instead my head dropped into my hands and I wept uncontrollably.

I didn't see it coming. But in that moment the grief I had buried came flooding to the surface.

Years of loss. Years of fear. Years of shrinking back from love because I didn't know whether I could survive another goodbye.

That day taught me something important: Sometimes trauma lies by telling you that pulling away protects you. But what it really does is rob you of presence. It tells you to leave first when what you really need to do is lean in.

And that is Misknowing too.

Not because I didn't love. But because fear had rearranged what I believed love could survive. She passed not long after. And while the pain was real, I was thankful I'd met it before she went. Because when we allow ourselves to fully feel, we don't just grieve a loss, we honor the love that made it hurt.

Take a moment before you move forward.

For Reflection

- Has loss—of a person, a relationship, a season—ever taught you to protect yourself in ways that now feel like isolation?
- Have you ever pulled back from love not because you didn't care but because you didn't want to feel the pain of it being taken away?
- Has your fear of what *might happen* kept you from being fully present in what *is happening*?

This is what trauma does. It makes fear feel wise. It makes distance feel safe. But now that you see it, you can start to release it.

And that's what we'll do next.

BREAKING THE AGREEMENT

Once you identify a Misknowing—a belief that was shaped by pain, not truth—you can't afford to live by it anymore.

Because every time you agree with the lie, you give it permission to shape your life. You make room for it in your decisions. You give it space in your relationships. You build around it. You bend around it. And eventually you become what the lie says you are.

But just because something shaped you doesn't mean it has the right to define you. The moment you recognize a lie, you have the power to break the agreement. And this is not just emotional work, it's spiritual warfare.

Earlier we talked about what Scripture calls strongholds: fortified arguments, false belief systems, mental structures that exalt themselves against the knowledge of God. Here's what Paul says about it: "For the weapons of our warfare are not carnal but mighty in God for pulling down strongholds, casting down arguments and every high thing that exalts itself against the knowledge of God" (2 Cor. 10:4–5). That's what Misknowing is. It's a high thing, exalting itself against the truth God has spoken about you.

But here's the good news: You have spiritual weapons. You have authority. You have power. Because you've been ordained. And that means you don't have to live by the lie another day.

Here's how we break the agreement:

1. *Identify the lie.* What did the trauma teach you to believe about yourself, others, or God?
2. *Expose the root.* Where did it come from? Who said it? What moment birthed it?
3. *Renounce the agreement.* Speak it out. Say, "I break agreement with the belief that . . ." And be specific. Be bold.

4. *Replace it with truth.* Not just any truth—divine Knowing. What does God say about you? What does the Word say? What does your spirit know is real, even if your pain tries to argue?

Here's why this is so important: You can't just stop believing a lie. You have to replace it. Because if you don't fill that space with truth, the lie will come back looking for a home.

That's why I created something for myself that I still use to this day. It's called an I AM statement. It's a declaration of who I am. Not based on feelings. Not based on trauma. Not based on performance. But based on truth. I read it daily, because I know the lies are persistent, but truth is more powerful.

We'll get to that in the next section.

But for now just remember this: You have the authority to break every agreement you never should've made. And you have the backing of heaven to establish new ones. You are not powerless. You are not stuck. You are ordained.

And it's time to start living like it.

RECLAIMING TRUE KNOWING

Healing isn't just about what you let go of. It's about what you pick up in its place.

You've identified the lies. You've traced them back to where they began. You've broken agreement with them. Now it's time to establish something stronger.

Because the work isn't over once you silence the lie. You have to rehearse the truth until it's louder, stronger, and deeper than anything pain ever taught you. Until it's automatic. That's what reclaiming true Knowing looks like. It's not a onetime realization. It's a daily rhythm. A choice to believe what God says, not what your fear, your past, or your pain has tried to whisper.

That's why I created my I AM statement, a personal declaration I read regularly to remind my soul who I am, not based on performance or pain but based on purpose.

It's how I fight. How I renew my mind. How I make sure that, every day, my spirit hears who I truly am.

I won't share it here in full, because it's personal. But I want to help you create your own. You'll find mine, along with other tools and resources, on my website, www.ToureRoberts.com/Knowing.

In the meantime, here's a version you can speak over yourself as a starting point:

I AM Statement

> I am called. I am chosen. I am secure in who I am and whose I am. I am not what happened to me. I am not what others said about me. I am whole. I am loved. I am seen. I am a son/daughter of God, ordained for greatness. I have divine insight, wisdom, and clarity. I am a door opener, a chain breaker, a kingdom builder. I don't shrink. I don't perform. I don't beg. I know who I am. And I walk in it, today and every day.

You can take this and make it your own. Make it personal. Make it powerful. Make it a sword you swing every morning when you rise. Because the truth is, you were never meant to live under the lies of trauma. You were born to live under the weight of divine Knowing.

And when you declare it, rehearse it, and live by it, you don't just feel free, you *are* free.

Let's pray:

God, thank you for shining your light into the places where we've walked in darkness. Thank you for meeting us in the pain, the memory, the silence, and calling us not just out but through.

We surrender every lie we've agreed with, every false narrative that has wrapped itself around our identity. We break agreement with shame. We break agreement with fear. We break agreement with every distorted truth trauma ever tried to teach us.

And now we make room for truth. Truth about who we are. Truth about who you are. Truth about what we carry and what we're here to release into the world.

Let your Spirit remind us daily that we are not our pain. We are not our past. We are not what we had to survive.

We are known. We are whole. We are becoming.

And we will walk in that truth, no matter what yesterday tried to tell us.

In Jesus' name, amen.

Now that you've released the lie, it's time to rise in the truth. You've done the hard work. You've named the lie. You've confronted the memory. You've reclaimed the truth.

Now walk in it.

When the lie tries to return, speak your truth. When shame whispers, remind it who you are. When trauma tries to resurface, remind yourself you are no longer living from that place.

You've been given divine tools. You've been armed with true Knowing. You are no longer reacting, you are responding from truth.

So don't shrink. Don't second-guess. Don't let what once shaped you define where you're going.

You are free. You are whole. You Know.

TEN

KNOWING, SEEING, SAYING

> Faith is the daring of the soul to go farther than it can see.
>
> —*William Newton Clarke*

THERE IS A KIND OF KNOWING THAT LEADS YOU BEYOND where your eyes can take you. It moves you past facts, past fear, past familiarity. This Knowing doesn't rely on evidence, it becomes the evidence.

Because when you truly know something, you don't wait for confirmation to believe it. You speak it. You move toward it. You begin to build with what hasn't shown up yet.

This is not wishful thinking. It's not hype. It's not blind hope. It's what Scripture calls faith.

THE CONNECTION BETWEEN KNOWING AND FAITH

> Now faith is the substance of things hoped for, the evidence of things not seen.
>
> —*Hebrews 11:1*

Faith is not a feeling. It's not a spiritual hunch or an emotional high. Faith is Knowing in motion. It is what happens when revelation takes root in your spirit and becomes more real to you than what you can see, touch, or explain.

It doesn't wait quietly in the background. It speaks. It moves. It acts. That's why Hebrews 11:3 begins with the phrase "by faith we understand." Faith gives you a kind of understanding that logic alone could never produce. It turns on what Scripture calls the eyes of your understanding—your spiritual eyes.

These are the eyes that allow you to perceive what hasn't happened yet and still believe it's already in motion. You were born with them. They've been with you all along. But just like candles sitting in a drawer during a blackout, you don't realize how much you need them until the lights you've trusted go out.

That's when faith shows up. That's when your Knowing turns on. That's when the voice of God speaks louder than your circumstances.

In *Purpose Awakening,* I talked about these spiritual eyes—how they're not just symbolic, they're strategic. They help you perceive what's already yours in the spirit before it becomes visible in the natural. They guide you toward what's been promised, even when the path hasn't fully appeared.

That's the power of Knowing. Because once you Know something deep in your spirit, you're no longer living based on sight. You're walking by faith. Not aimlessly, not blindly, but by the inner awareness that what God said is already complete, even if it hasn't arrived in your timeline yet.

Faith doesn't create from nothing. It partners with what already exists in God's mind and pulls it into view.

That's why Knowing always comes first. Because you can't say what you don't know. And you won't see what you've never had the courage to declare.

Faith is the bridge between the invisible and the inevitable. And the moment you know what God has said about you—and dare to believe it—you've already started the process of making it real.

THE POWER OF WORDS

This is where we shift from the internal Knowing to the external expression—the spoken word.

Because once you know something, you have a responsibility to speak like you know it.

In the spiritual realm, words are not filler, words are force. They don't just inform. They create. They don't just describe what is. They help shape what will be.

The writer of Hebrews puts it this way: "By faith we understand that the worlds were framed by the word of God" (Heb. 11:3). The word translated "framed" here is powerful. In the Greek, it means to complete thoroughly, to align, arrange, and finish with intention.

That means the universe didn't just appear, it was spoken into order. God didn't build the world with his hands. He built it with his voice. He said, "Let there be . . ." and everything obeyed. The stars. The galaxies. The boundaries of oceans. The seed within fruit. The breath within lungs. The word of God didn't just describe creation, it delivered it. And you were made in that image.

That means your words, when aligned with divine truth, carry a kind of spiritual creative power too. Proverbs 18:21 tells us, "Death and life are in the power of the tongue." That's not poetry. That's law. And it means that what you say has the power to:

- Build or break
- Advance or delay
- Align or detour

Your voice is a vessel. And every time you speak what you know, you give life to that Knowing in the physical realm.

That's why silence can be dangerous. It's not just that you're not saying anything, it's that you're not releasing what's true. And when you don't release it, you delay the manifestation of what God has revealed.

You may know you're called. You may know you're healed. You may know God has provided. You may know you're not average, that your life carries purpose and power. But if you won't say it, you'll never see it.

Because God framed the world with words, and so will you.

WHAT ARE YOU SPEAKING INTO?

Before you move on, take a moment to reflect.

Is there something in your life you've been tearing down with your words that you've actually been called to build up? Maybe it's a child. A spouse. Your career. Your calling. A problem that feels too big to change, so you've chosen to speak from frustration instead of faith.

Whatever it is, what would it look like to speak life into that place instead?

Ask God to show you where your words need to shift. And commit, starting today, to speak only what aligns with what you know, not what you fear.

THE SEQUENCE: KNOWING → SAYING → SEEING

There's a pattern to how faith works. It starts as a whisper inside of you. A truth that clicks in your spirit so deeply, so undeniably you just know it didn't come from you. That's the first part: Knowing.

But Knowing isn't where it ends. In fact, Knowing was never meant to stay silent. Once you truly Know something, it begins to rise in your language. In your tone. In your declarations. In your prayers. In your conversations. You start to speak what you Know not because it's visible yet but because it's already real to you.

That's the second part: saying. And when you keep saying what you Know, even when it looks like nothing's changing, something shifts. Atmospheres respond. Doors open. Provision finds you. Ideas become reality. What was invisible materializes. That's the final part: seeing.

This is the divine sequence: Knowing → Saying → Seeing.

- Knowing is about believing at the deepest level that what God has revealed is true.
- Saying is using your words in agreement with your Knowing.
- Seeing is what happens when what God has ordained and revealed has been made manifest, moving from a promise made to a promise fulfilled.

And if you skip one step, you'll always feel stuck.

Some people try to say what they don't really know, and it feels forced, flat, fragile. Others know the truth but won't say it because they're afraid of being disappointed. Afraid of looking foolish. Afraid of jinxing what they were born to release.

But if you want to see what God has shown you, you have to speak from the place of what you Know, not what you see.

Let's go back to someone we've talked about before: Abraham.

Before he became Abraham, his name was Abram. Abram was a man God chose not because he had it all together but because he was willing to follow God into something he couldn't yet see.

God gave him a promise: "You will be the father of many nations."

There was just one problem: Abram didn't have any children. He and his wife Sarah were well past childbearing years, and everything in the natural world said it was too late. Too far gone. Impossible.

But God didn't flinch. He didn't adjust the promise. He didn't apologize for how unbelievable it sounded. Instead, he gave Abram a new name—Abraham, which literally means "father of many."

"As it is written: 'I have made you a father of many nations'" (Rom. 4:17 NIV). Notice the language: Not "I will." Not "maybe someday." But "I have." God speaks in completed terms, even when the evidence hasn't shown up yet.

And here's what's important: Abraham had to start calling himself by that name long before he saw the child, long before nations came from his bloodline, long before the promise manifested.

Can you imagine that? Introducing yourself as "Hi, I'm the father of many" when you don't have even one child?

But that's the language of faith. That's what it looks like to say what you Know before you see it. Abraham had to walk into every room, every conversation, every prayer in agreement with the promise. And eventually what he said became what he saw.

So here's the question: What has God shown you that you haven't had the courage to say? What truth is living in your spirit but hasn't made it to your lips?

You've been shown. You've been told. You've been marked.

Now you must speak.

Because until you speak what you Know, you'll never see what you were promised.

SPEAKING IN UNCOMFORTABLE ENVIRONMENTS

It's one thing to declare something in your journal or behind closed doors. It's another to say it out loud when your environment doesn't affirm it yet. When the room is quiet. When the people around you don't understand the vision. When your circumstances don't line up with your confession.

This is where Knowing meets resistance. And the only way through it is to say it anyway.

It's easy to speak what you Know when everything around you agrees. When the numbers make sense. When the opportunity is visible. When the people in the room already believe what you believe.

But what about the moments when your surroundings haven't caught up with your revelation? What about when your bank account contradicts the promise? When the doctor's report clashes with the word you've received? When you're praying in faith but the room still smells like failure?

This is where boldness is born. This is where you learn what faith really feels like. This is where saying is tested. There will be moments—if you haven't lived through them already—when the pressure to stay silent feels overwhelming. You'll know what God said. You'll feel it in your bones. But saying it out loud will feel like a risk. What if I sound arrogant? What if they think I'm crazy? What if nothing changes?

But here's the truth: If you say what you Know only when it's comfortable, you'll never see what you've been promised when it's costly. Sometimes the most powerful thing you can do is declare the truth in a space that hasn't seen it yet.

Jesus modeled this constantly. He would walk into rooms full of unbelief and still speak like heaven had the final word. He declared healing in atmospheres of resistance. He spoke peace into violent storms. He called Lazarus—a man who had been dead for four days—out of the tomb in front of a crowd that was already planning the burial.

They told him it was too late. They told him the body would

stink. They told him the story was over. But Jesus stood in front of the grave, looked at what was lifeless, and spoke anyway.

Why?

Because truth doesn't wait for agreement, it speaks to create alignment.

You may not feel like your voice carries that kind of power. But it does. When you speak what you Know, even in rooms of tension or silence, you do more than release words, you plant seeds. Seeds that carry the blueprint of what God has revealed. Seeds that push back against doubt. Seeds that shift atmospheres, even when no one else sees the shift happening.

So say it when you're unsure. Say it when it makes no sense. Say it when you're surrounded by doubt. Say it when you feel the pushback. Say it when you're the only one speaking faith in the room. Say it anyway.

Because silence doesn't protect your promise. Speech does.

And every time you speak from a place of Knowing, you're declaring, "He said it. I believe it. And I won't shrink back—no matter where I am."

Take a moment to think about a room that once made you shrink. An environment where you went quiet, even though you knew what God had said. A moment when you backed down from your boldness because the room felt too cold, too big, too unfamiliar.

Now, what would it look like to walk back into that same kind of space not with fear but with Knowing?

Where's the one place you've been quiet that now needs to hear your voice? Make a commitment today: "The next time I enter that space, I will not shrink. I will speak."

Because your silence won't change the room. But your voice might.

ACTIVATING THE SEQUENCE: LIVING WHAT YOU KNOW

Faith isn't just a feeling, it's a force. But that force doesn't activate on its own. It responds to your participation.

The Knowing → Saying → Seeing sequence isn't just a spiritual concept, it's a creative rhythm, and like any rhythm it must be practiced. Cultivated. Lived.

If you want to see the fruit of what you Know, you have to engage the process with intention. Here are a few ways to begin living this sequence not just conceptually but powerfully and practically:

1. START YOUR DAY WITH A KNOWING MOMENT

Don't just wake up and scroll. Wake up and settle. Settle into what you Know.

Before you let the world speak, give the knower inside you the first word.

How to Practice It

Choose a phrase, Scripture, or divine truth that resonates in your spirit. Speak it. Write it. Anchor yourself in it before you engage with the noise of the world.

Why It Matters

The beginning of the day is when your spirit is most open. Seeding it with divine truth gives your faith a foundation to stand on.

Example

I Know I'm guided. I Know I'm covered. I Know my steps are ordered—even the ones that don't yet make sense.

2. SPEAK LIKE YOU BELIEVE IT

Words create worlds. That's not poetry, that's spiritual law. If you've received divine Knowing, it's your responsibility to give it voice.

How to Practice It

Craft bold declarations based on what you Know. Don't just think them, speak them out loud. Speak them over your day, your body, your work, your future.

Why It Matters

Saying aligns the atmosphere with the revelation that Knowing provided. It doesn't just reinforce your faith, it shifts the environment.

Example

What I carry is bigger than what I see. I'm walking in divine timing, provision, and favor.

3. MOVE LIKE IT'S ALREADY HAPPENING

Knowing without motion is potential without power. Once you've Known and said, you've got to move—even if the move is small.

How to Practice It

Take one step that aligns with what you've declared. Make the call. Write the page. Build the outline. Send the email. Don't wait for the stars to align, start moving like you're already under an open heaven.

Why It Matters

Movement is a prophetic act. It signals to your spirit—and to the world—that you're not just dreaming, you're building.

4. SHOW UP AUTHENTICALLY EVERYWHERE

Faith doesn't shrink to fit a room. If you Know something, let it shape how you show up—everywhere.

How to Practice It

Whether in boardrooms, classrooms, or casual spaces, let what you Know inform how you speak, lead, and love. Don't hide your light to make others comfortable.

Why It Matters

The power of Knowing isn't just personal, it's influential. When you live out loud, you invite others to do the same.

5. STAY IN ALIGNMENT DURING THE WAIT

The hardest part of this sequence isn't the Knowing or the saying. It's the waiting to see.

But delays don't mean denials, they just test your alignment.

How to Practice It

Keep showing up. Keep speaking. Keep walking, even if you don't yet see results. Your consistency under pressure is often the bridge to breakthrough.

Why It Matters

Many people give up in the "almost." But if God spoke it, and you Know it, you can't let silence make you question what was spoken in clarity.

This sequence isn't magic. It's movement. It's partnership with the divine.

And when you live it—when you activate what you Know by

saying and seeing it through—it doesn't just change your life, it reshapes your world.

KEEP SPEAKING UNTIL YOU SEE

The hardest part of faith is not always starting. Sometimes it's staying.

It's easy to say what you Know right after the revelation hits. In the heat of a moment, after a powerful word, when you're surrounded by worship, prophecy, or clarity, your voice rises without hesitation.

But what about after that moment? What about when days turn into weeks? When the silence feels long, when the evidence feels delayed, when your declaration starts sounding like a broken record?

This is where many people stop. Not because they don't believe but because they expected to see faster.

But here's what you need to know: Your words are working. Every time you speak what you Know, you're reinforcing a spiritual blueprint. You're continuing the construction of what's being built, even when the site looks empty.

Faith is not just a onetime statement. It's a steady rhythm. A daily alignment. A spiritual echo that keeps declaring, "I haven't changed my mind because God hasn't changed his."

Think of your words like rain. Each declaration nourishes the seed. It may take time before anything breaks the surface, but that doesn't mean growth isn't happening underground.

So don't stop speaking just because you're tired. Don't stop declaring just because it's quiet. Don't let delay break your agreement. Say it until the atmosphere shifts. Say it until your body responds. Say it until your mind aligns. Say it until the resources show up. Say it until the promise is standing right in front of you.

And when you see it, you'll realize it didn't start that day. It started the moment you Knew. It accelerated the moment you said. And it manifested as you kept saying—until you saw.

And what comes next? It's the part you've been waiting for. You've spoken it. You've planted the seed. You've declared what you Know. And now you're entering the season of unfolding.

This is what your faith has been leading you to—not just the moment you see it all at once but the moment you start seeing it come alive, piece by piece. The unfolding is where heaven's yes starts showing up in time. It's where doors open, alignments happen, resources find you, and confirmations rise like the sun breaking through the clouds after a long night.

In the next chapter we'll talk about what it looks like to live in the beauty of that process, the unfolding of Knowing. Because what you've Known and what you've said is finally beginning to take shape. And if you stay in agreement with what's been revealed, you will see it happen in ways that exceed what you ever dared to imagine.

Let's step into it.

ELEVEN

THE UNFOLDING OF KNOWING

For the earnest expectation of the creation eagerly waits for the revealing of the sons of God.

—Romans 8:19

IMAGINE WALKING THROUGH A HOUSE YOU'VE INHERited. From the outside, it looks beautiful. Well built. Complete. A gift, fully formed. But as you explore, you realize there's more than meets the eye.

A hallway you hadn't noticed before. A staircase tucked behind a door. Rooms that seem to appear only as you keep walking. A story that wasn't on the blueprint, or maybe one you just couldn't see until now. You begin to understand: This isn't just a house, it's a mansion. And with every step you take, you're not building it, you're discovering it.

That's what Knowing feels like as it unfolds.

What God placed inside of you was never small. It was never limited to one room, one moment, or one dimension. Your identity, your gifts, your purpose, your calling, all of it was built into you before time began. But it doesn't show up all at once. It arrives in stages. Revealed as you walk. Uncovered as you obey. Discovered as you grow.

Everything you will ever be, everything you are becoming was planted in you as seed.

And now, day by day, that seed is opening.

UNDERSTANDING THE NATURE OF UNFOLDING

Knowing doesn't always arrive fully formed. It's not a light switch, it's a sunrise. A gradual revealing. A truth that deepens as you continue to walk with it.

Just because you've received a revelation doesn't mean you've seen all of it yet. Revelation is often layered. What you knew then was true—but what you Know now has expanded it. And what you'll Know tomorrow will stretch it even farther.

Knowing unfolds.

Think of a flower. Tightly wrapped. Full of potential. All the beauty already exists inside the bud, but it's hidden—for now. It blooms not because it was incomplete but because the conditions were right.

That's how Knowing works.

God isn't waiting for your revelation to get bigger, he's waiting for *you* to grow into the capacity to hold it. What you've received isn't wrong. It's not broken. It's not a mistake. It's just still opening. You are in process. But that doesn't mean you're off track. It means you're becoming. And the becoming is just as holy as the arriving.

Everything God has spoken over your life, everything you are sensing, hoping, reaching for, already exists in seed form. The calling. The clarity. The confidence. The impact. The voice. The presence. The bigness. It's in you. But it won't all show up at once. It unfolds.

We often equate "now" with "real." If I can see it now, it's real. If I can hold it now, it's real. But there are things that are just as real even when they're still becoming visible. That promise? Still real. That word? Still valid. That vision? Still alive. That dream? Still unfolding.

The mistake many people make is assuming that if it hasn't fully shown up yet, then maybe it wasn't real to begin with. But the flower in the bud is just as real as the flower in full bloom. The promise you carry is still alive even if it hasn't unfolded yet. The Knowing you received years ago still holds weight even if you don't see the full picture.

Because the nature of divine Knowing is that it reveals itself over time.

Not because God is hiding from you. But because he's walking with you. He unfolds what he knows in step with your transformation. If he were to show it all to you at once, you might run from it or try to build it before you're ready to sustain it. So instead he gives it to you in stages. Layer by layer. Season by season. Until what's been planted in you looks like what's been spoken over you.

Let's take a moment to reflect on some questions.

For Reflection

- What if the delays haven't been detours but divine pacing?
- What if what you're waiting to see is actually already alive, just waiting for the right season to open?

THE GIFT OF BECOMING

One of the greatest gifts you'll ever receive is the revelation that you're not being made from scratch. You're being revealed.

There is more in you than you've seen. More than others have recognized. More than your past can explain. And more than your present can fully contain.

You are not being made up. You're being unfolded.

You're not a random spark. You are the continuation of a divine thought. A vision that heaven agreed upon long before time started ticking. And as you unfold, something extraordinary happens in the universe. "For the creation waits in eager expectation for the children of God to be revealed" (Rom. 8:19 NIV).

Creation isn't just a backdrop. It's not passive scenery. Creation is alive. It has personality. It has desire. It has expectation. And it's not just waiting on your becoming, it's holding the materials for it. Creation is pregnant with the resources needed to bring your calling to life. Everything God designed for your journey—the relationships, the timing, the provisions, the platforms—is coded into the world around you, waiting on your emergence.

And the moment you begin to walk into who you truly are, creation doesn't just observe, it responds. When you become, so does creation.

This is the divine choreography of unfolding.

You move in faith, and the path appears beneath your feet. "The steps of a good man are ordered by the LORD, and He delights in his way" (Ps. 37:23). That word "ordered" in Hebrew means to erect. To build. To establish. That means your steps aren't just guided, they are architected in real time. As you walk, the ground rises to meet you. As you move forward, what's needed to support your next step rises to hold the weight of your becoming.

You are not stepping out onto nothing. You're stepping into something God designed to catch you. And this is why you feel what you feel. That pressure. That sense of more. The quiet discontent that whispers, *I'm not done yet.*

You're not crazy. You're not off track. You're not being ungrateful for what is.

You're simply sensing the truth: You're still unfolding.

Everything God has deposited in you has a time and place for its revealing. It's not all meant to be revealed at once. Some truths take years to grow into. Some doors stay closed until you're strong enough to walk through them with character. Some promises are so big that God protects you from the weight of them until you're developed enough to carry it.

You're not behind schedule. You're being built into the schedule. So give yourself permission to become. Permission to be in process. Permission to honor what's forming, even when you can't explain it.

Because what's forming isn't just about you. It's about the world waiting to receive you. Creation has been holding its breath, waiting for you to rise. Waiting for you to own who you are. And when you do, it will respond. It will unlock. It will release.

Not because you forced it. But because it was always meant for the version of you that's emerging now.

ENCOURAGEMENT FOR THE IN-BETWEEN

There is a space between revelation and fulfillment that can feel like a wilderness.

It's not where you started, but it's not yet where you saw yourself ending up. It's the space between what God said and what you can see. And if you're not careful, this space can make you question everything. Did I hear wrong? Did I miss the timing? Did I do something to mess it up? Was that even God? But here's the truth: The in-between is not a mistake. It's part of the unfolding.

God is not just developing the promise, he's developing you.

And that means there will be days when you're still holding the word but not yet holding the outcome. There will be seasons when it feels like your obedience got you silence. Like your faith is building something invisible. Like your progress is internal, not external.

That's not failure. That's formation.

This space, this in-between, is holy ground. It's where roots go deep. It's where trust is built. It's where motives are purified and strength is refined. If the promise arrived before your character was ready to hold it, you'd risk building something too heavy to sustain. So God unfolds you slowly. Not to punish you but to prepare you.

Even Jesus had an in-between. Thirty years of preparation for three years of public ministry. The Son of God hidden in plain sight. But nothing was wasted. Not one moment. Everything was part of the plan, even the waiting.

So if you're in between, you're not lost. You're not overlooked. You're on track. And the track is unfolding beneath your feet even when it looks like nothing is moving.

WHAT'S YOUR IN-BETWEEN?

Take a moment here. Be honest with yourself. What is your in-between right now?

Where are you waiting, not because you've done something wrong but because something in you is still unfolding? What word are you holding that hasn't yet become what you can see?

Now that you understand that this isn't delay but divine development, how will you walk through it differently? What does commitment to this part of the process look like now that you know it's sacred?

Write it down. Pray it through. Say it aloud.

Your posture in the middle can shape the strength of your arrival.

CHANGING THE WAY YOU SEE DELAY

Delay is one of the most misunderstood parts of the process. We often assume that when something takes longer than expected, it means something has gone wrong.

But delay doesn't always mean denial. Sometimes delay is divine pacing. Sometimes delay is development. And sometimes delay is alignment—God orchestrating timing, maturity, and conditions so the promise arrives in power, not pressure.

We live in a world that glorifies fast. Quick results. Instant validation. Overnight success. But in the economy of God, the process is as holy as the promise. God doesn't just give the blessing, he prepares the vessel.

There's something I've always known about myself: I was supposed to be an author.

Not just a content creator. Not just a preacher who could write. But someone who would release words—words that would outlive me. Words that would find people I'd never meet. Words that would go where I could not go.

I could feel it. It lived in me.

And yet, for years, it didn't happen.

I had starts and stops—moments when I put some thoughts on paper, but nothing ever materialized. Life was moving fast. I was growing a church, growing a family, growing as a leader. And though I never let go of what I Knew, I had almost stopped looking for it.

Then one day, seemingly out of nowhere, a young woman approached me after service. There was fire in her eyes and conviction in her voice. She said, "There's a book in you. And I can help you get it out."

Turns out she worked at a literary agency. And just like that, I realized—this was a moment. A manifestation moment.

God always has someone or something assigned to midwife the baby you've been carrying.

We worked together to shape what would become my very first book. It was my introduction to the world as an author. And when we were ready, we pitched it to publishers and landed a deal with one of the biggest publishing houses in the world.

Yet that was just the beginning.

The book you're holding now? It's my fourth.

It was always in me. But it had to unfold. Not because I wasn't ready to write but because the fullness of the moment required timing, maturity, and divine alignment. That's what delay really is. Not punishment. Not distance. But preparation.

God doesn't rush greatness. And he doesn't allow what's meant to be lasting to be built too fast. When you understand this, you stop fighting delay and start partnering with the process. You start trusting the rhythm of heaven instead of comparing your pace to someone else's. You begin to realize that delay isn't passive, it's pregnant.

And when the time is right, what you've Known, what you've spoken, will unfold.

A CALL TO PERSEVERANCE

Some people's callings seem to catch fire quickly.

They launch and rise like rockets, gaining momentum and visibility in what feels like an instant. And it's tempting to think, *That's how it's supposed to happen.*

But I've learned something over the years: The weight of what's coming will always require a foundation strong enough to carry it. And sometimes that foundation takes time.

When I started in ministry, I didn't explode onto the scene. I didn't have a massive platform. I didn't step into crowds and cameras. I started with a few people. A small room. A quiet conviction that God was calling me to something big.

And that's what made it hard.

Because while I was ministering in one room, I was carrying a vision that felt like a nation. I knew I was called to the world. To inspire people across cultures, industries, and generations. But for a long time my outside didn't match my inside. I carried grace on a global level while living out faith on a local one.

And I'll be honest: There were moments when it felt like I'd missed something. Like maybe I'd misheard. Like maybe my pace was too slow. I'd look around and see others rising fast. Their ministries taking off, their platforms expanding—and meanwhile I was still building, brick by brick. I even envied some of them at times.

But then I noticed something. Some of those fast risers began to fall.

With the same speed that lifted them, they were brought back down. And I realized that there's a difference between growing tall and growing deep. There is a grace in the slow build. Because while your gift might open the door, only your character can keep you in the room.

And God, in his mercy, was using those early years to grow me internally. To build my leadership. To deepen my wisdom. To increase my capacity. To strengthen my ability to stand under what I was called to stand over.

Now, all of these years later, we minister to millions of people in more than 150 nations around the world. The same grace I felt in that small room I'm now walking in on a global scale. But it didn't happen all at once. It unfolded. And if I would've given up when it looked small, I would've forfeited the bigness I carry now.

So hear me: If it's slow, stay with it. If it's quiet, keep speaking. If it's hidden, keep building. Because, as Solomon wrote, "better is the end of a thing than the beginning" (Eccl. 7:8 KJV). The goal is not to start fast. It's to finish full.

And if you refuse to quit, you will see what you've been carrying come into view.

TRUSTING GOD'S TIMING

One of the most important lessons in the unfolding is learning to trust the timing. Not just trusting the promise. Not just trusting the Knowing. But trusting when—and how—it comes to pass.

Because the things God speaks over your life aren't just true, they're timed. And sometimes the hardest part is trusting what you heard when what you're seeing hasn't caught up yet.

Fifteen years ago I sensed something stir in my spirit. It wasn't loud. It wasn't dramatic. It was subtle, but weighty. It was a Knowing: *You're called to Africa*. I didn't go searching for it. I didn't manufacture it. It came to me.

And I knew not just that I would minister there but that I would do business there. That somehow I would be part of the renewal, the innovation, the forward movement of an entire continent. But at the time I had no relationships in Africa. I'd never even been there. I had no direct access to the vision I had received.

Still, I held the Knowing.

And over the years, something interesting began to happen. I started checking my social media metrics. And slowly but surely, Africa became my top audience when broken down by city. Lagos, Nigeria; Accra, Ghana; and others were outranking cities in the United States. Then I noticed my podcast beginning to chart in multiple African nations, sometimes even hitting number one in the category of business and entrepreneurship.

I couldn't explain it. But I knew God was up to something. And then the doors started opening.

First we were invited to minister in Nigeria. Then in South Africa, where tens of thousands came. Arenas packed. Hearts ready. Voices lifted. People welcoming us like we were already family. It wasn't just about ministry. It was legacy. It was purpose. It was prophecy.

And then a new kind of door opened.

I was scrolling on social media one day when I saw a familiar face, an old friend I hadn't spoken to in years. He was in Ghana, doing business. It hit me: I'd known he was Ghanaian, and I'd known he was a businessman based in the States, but I had never connected those dots until that moment.

That was the spark.

I reached out. We talked. We prayed. He introduced me to key people in Ghana—leaders, advisers, builders. And doors began opening in business, ministry, government.

Now, at the time of this writing, I have a trip scheduled to meet with the president, to minister and to explore kingdom-minded investment opportunities on the continent. What started as a whisper fifteen years ago is now becoming a movement.

Sometimes the purpose for a relationship isn't immediately obvious. It's not about what someone can do for you in the moment. It's about timing. That's why it's so important to honor your connections. To treat people well. To lead with integrity. Because character shows up in how you treat someone you don't think can help you. And in the economy of God, you never know who God will use to unlock what's been hidden inside you.

That's how the timing of God works.

It's not always fast. It's rarely predictable. But it's always perfect. And when it happens, you realize that the delay wasn't a punishment. It was positioning. Because some things are so big, so multilayered, so globally connected that they take time to align.

So if you're still holding a promise that hasn't manifested yet, don't rush it. Don't force it. Don't panic. Just walk in step with the Spirit. Let God order your path. And trust that every relationship, every revelation, every opportunity will arrive when it's supposed to.

And when it does, you won't have to chase it, you'll walk right into it.

CAN YOU TRUST THE TIMING?

Think about something you've been waiting on. A word. A door. A relationship. A vision that hasn't materialized—yet.

Now ask yourself, Have I trusted the promise but struggled to trust the pace?

What if the delay isn't rejection but preparation? What if the relationship you've been wondering about isn't irrelevant, it's just not ready yet?

Can you give God permission to align the timing, not just the outcome? Can you trust that even silence can be a sign that heaven is setting something up?

Write it down. Pray through it. Open your hands. And declare, "I trust you, Lord, even in the waiting."

LIVING WITH EXPECTANCY

You don't have to see the full picture to live like something beautiful is unfolding. You don't have to know the timeline to trust the process. And you don't have to have the blueprint to believe that what's next is already in motion.

Because once you know God, once you've walked with him long enough to see how he plants, waters, aligns, and reveals, you can rest in this truth: The best is not behind you. It's ahead of you. And it's unfolding—right now.

Expectancy is not hype. It's not emotional energy or wishful thinking. It's not positive vibes. It's not forced optimism.

Expectancy is a posture.

It's the stance of someone who understands that heaven has a plan and God is never late. It's the mindset of a person who wakes up every day looking for the next layer to be revealed.

It's not about striving. It's about watching. Waiting not passively but prophetically.

This is how you live when you understand the rhythm of the Spirit. You stop panicking. You stop measuring yourself against others. You stop forcing what's not ready. And instead you lean in. You live prepared. You live available. You live in step with grace. "The path of the righteous is like the morning sun, shining ever brighter till the full light of day" (Prov. 4:18 NIV). That means your journey isn't dimming. It's growing in brilliance. One step at a time.

So if it's quiet right now, stay expectant.

If the doors aren't swinging open yet, stay expectant.

If you're still carrying the Knowing without a full picture, stay expectant.

Because God is not done. Not even close.

And when it unfolds, you'll look back and realize that this was the part of the story where everything was being positioned. You'll see how the silence was setting the stage. How the delay was buying time for deeper roots. How the people, the opportunities, the resources were all being assigned to your arrival.

So keep walking. Keep watching. Keep waking up with expectation. Because what God started, he intends to finish. And the life you were born to live is still opening layer by layer, moment by moment, Knowing by Knowing.

It's unfolding.

And you're right on time.

Creation has not given up on you. Heaven has not forgotten you. And everything is still working together for good, because the one who called you is still calling.

And now as you continue to walk in what's unfolding, there's one more step.

It's time to take everything you've Known—everything you've declared, believed, and waited for—and bring it into how you live. Not perfectly. But practically. Intentionally. Daily. Because Knowing was never meant to be a concept. It was always meant to become your confidence. Your anchor. Your peace.

And in the final chapter we'll learn how to make it just that.

We don't just carry certainty. We practice it.

TWELVE

PRACTICING CERTAINTY

> And we know that in all things God works for the good of those who love him, who have been called according to his purpose.
>
> —*Romans 8:28 NIV*

CERTAINTY ISN'T SOMETHING YOU REACH. IT'S SOMETHING you practice.

Because life isn't static. It shifts. It throws curveballs. It erupts without warning. The economy contracts. Politics divide. Nations rage. Wildfires spread. Floodwaters rise. Earthquakes shake. News cycles trigger fear. And the future feels harder to predict than ever.

One day it's a market crash. The next it's a school shooting. A new war breaks out overseas while layoffs roll in at home. Grocery bills go up. Gas prices fluctuate. And families—average, hardworking families—are doing everything they can just to make it from paycheck to paycheck.

We are living in a time when the world often feels like it's unraveling. And yet we are not called to collapse with it. We are called to stand in Knowing.

This final chapter is not about ignoring reality. It's not about pretending the world isn't unpredictable, unstable, or unjust. It's about learning how to live with peace, boldness, and alignment right in the middle of it.

Not because the world is predictable but because your foundation is immovable. You don't walk in certainty because everything makes sense. You walk in certainty because of what you Know.

And what you Know—if it's truly divine—won't change, even if everything else does.

So what does it mean to practice certainty?

It's not being perfect. It's not pretending to have it all together. It's not walking through life untouched by hardship, grief, or confusion. Practicing certainty means aligning your life with what God has revealed—daily. It's waking up and saying, "I don't know what the day holds, but I Know who holds me, and that's enough for me to keep walking."

It means that when chaos swirls, you choose peace. When the headlines scream, you choose perspective. When the world gets louder, you get quieter, returning to what you Know in your spirit and letting that steer the wheel of your decisions.

Practicing certainty is like exercising a muscle. It gets stronger the more you use it. You begin to live less by reaction and more by revelation. You stop waiting for everything around you to stabilize and start building from what's already been established within you. In a world that's shaking, stability becomes a superpower.

We are not practicing certainty because we're in denial. We're practicing it because we've been called. And Romans 8:28 assures us that if we are walking in our divine purpose, everything—everything—is working together for our good. That means even if you don't know how, even if it doesn't feel good right now, even if it looks like the world is falling apart, if you are walking in purpose, you are walking toward good.

This is the great promise of Knowing: that no matter how uncertain the world becomes, we are getting back to good. Not just eventually. Not just someday. But here. Now. In process. In motion. In practice.

Let's learn how to live like it.

CERTAINTY AS A SUPERPOWER

Certainty doesn't make life easier. It makes you stronger.

It doesn't eliminate conflict, chaos, or confusion, but it keeps those things from running your life. Certainty is a superpower, because while the world is reacting, you're anchored.

When you practice certainty, you don't crumble when your plans change. You don't unravel when the unexpected hits. You don't shrink back when the path gets cloudy.

You may feel it. You may wobble for a moment. You may even question things briefly. But you don't live there. Because you've built your life on something deeper than emotion or circumstances. Jesus described this kind of stability in Matthew 7: "Everyone who hears these words of mine and puts them into practice is like a wise man who built his house on the rock. The rain came down, the streams rose, and the winds blew and beat against that house; yet it did not fall, because it had its foundation on the rock" (vv. 24–25 NIV). The winds came. The storm beat against it. There was shaking, rattling, and pressure from every side. But the house didn't fall. Why? Because it was built on what was Known.

That's certainty.

And here's what's even more incredible—Jesus didn't say "understands these words" or "believes these words." He said "puts them into practice." What you build on Knowing, you must also practice. Not occasionally. Not conceptually. But consistently. Intentionally. Every single day.

Certainty is how you sleep in storms. How you lead with peace when everyone else is panicking. How you keep your hands on the wheel when your surroundings say to jump ship.

It's how Jesus stood before the cross, knowing the suffering was real, but also knowing the resurrection was already written.

That's what certainty does.

It doesn't pretend away the pain. It simply knows how the story ends.

When you live in certainty, you can:

- Wait without panicking.
- Love without clinging.
- Lead without performing.
- Speak with authority even when your surroundings say otherwise.

You stop asking, "What if I fall?" and start saying, "Even if I shake, I won't collapse." You stop living like everything could fall apart at any moment and start living like you were built to last.

Certainty shifts your posture.

You no longer need the room to agree with you before you move. You don't need applause to know you're on the right track. You don't need every variable figured out before you take your next step. You move because you Know. You speak because you Know. You stay steady because you Know.

And when that Knowing is rooted in God, nothing—nothing—can knock you off your path.

WHEN LIFE DOESN'T GO AS PLANNED

There will be days when what you Know is tested by what you see.

There will be moments when life takes a turn you didn't

anticipate and everything in you wants to throw up your hands and say, "What was all that Knowing for, anyway?"

Let's be honest. Disappointment is real. Loss is real. Mistakes happen. Doors close. People walk away. Plans unravel. And it's in those moments that certainty feels the most fragile.

But here's what I want you to understand: Certainty doesn't mean perfection. It means alignment.

You can be aligned with truth and still have a setback. You can be walking in purpose and still face pain. You can be fully certain and still find yourself in a moment that makes you question everything.

And when that happens, you have a choice: Will you let the moment rewrite what you Know? Or will you let what you Know recenter you in the moment?

Mistakes don't cancel out your Knowing. They reveal where your Knowing still needs to mature. Disappointments don't disqualify you. They train your eyes to look deeper, to see beyond what broke and recognize what's still standing.

And when you fall short—because we all do—certainty gives you something to come back to. It says, "I may have missed it, but I haven't lost it. I may have gotten shaken, but the foundation didn't move."

I've lived this.

I mentioned that years ago I went through a divorce. And although I knew it was the right decision—although it gave me a sense of authenticity and freedom—part of me was still crushed. Devastated. Uncertain.

I had believed for a miracle. I had faith that God could turn it around. That he could make my marriage something it never was. And when it didn't happen, I was heartbroken. I questioned everything.

Was I disqualified now? Would I be able to stand under the pressure of being a successful single man in a luring, seductive city? Was I still called? Was I still chosen? Was my future downgraded because of my disappointment?

Some voices around me, especially in religious circles, only amplified those fears. Their opinions weren't always kind, and they certainly weren't healing.

And then came the heaviest question of all: What about my children? Would this break them? Would this undo all my efforts to be to them what my father couldn't be to me?

It was the darkest season of my life.

That in-between we talked about earlier? This was it. I was living it. But in the midst of it all, there was still a sensing. A whisper. A Knowing. And when the darkness got deep, I leaned in to it. And that Knowing slowly, gently began to lead me into an unfolding truth I never could have imagined.

What I didn't realize then was that my relationship with my children wouldn't grow weaker after the divorce. It would grow stronger. I became more present. More intentional. More engaged. They no longer had to witness strife in the home. We didn't have to pretend. And the time I spent with them became time that was rooted in truth, peace, and connection.

And just when I thought maybe this would be my story—a single father, a pastor, a leader, doing the best he could alone—God revealed what he had been preparing for me all along.

A woman. From the South. With a heart so profound and a love so deep I didn't even know to ask for it.

She became my partner in purpose. My companion in calling. Someone who not only believed in me but saw me—and let me see her. And together we've done things I never could've imagined doing alone. Together we've built something extraordinary.

She had two children—beautiful souls—who needed a father. And I had three children who needed to see what healing love looked like. Together we became a family. A blended picture of restoration and grace. And as if that wasn't enough, God gave us a child together—a sign that new beginnings were still possible.

And even my ex-wife discovered her own wholeness, a freedom she may never have found if we had stayed where we were.

Things didn't go as I'd planned. But they were in God's plan. "'For my thoughts are not your thoughts, neither are your ways my ways,' declares the LORD" (Isa. 55:8 NIV). Sometimes the way God brings to pass what he's shown you is nothing like the way you would have chosen.

But that's the brilliance of his sovereignty.

And that's why certainty matters, because you won't always understand the route. But you can still trust the one who wrote the map.

Practicing certainty doesn't protect you from every storm. But it gives you something solid to stand on when the wind shows up.

You don't throw away what God revealed just because life got hard. You return to it. You reset. You realign. You rebuild. Certainty is what lets you say, "I didn't expect this, but I'm not undone. I'm still called. I still Know. And I'm still moving forward."

WHAT DIDN'T GO AS PLANNED?

Take a moment to reflect.

Was there a moment in your life that left you disoriented? Something that didn't go as you had hoped and left you feeling like the plan was ruined?

Did a disappointment—a divorce, a delay, a closed door—quietly convince you that what God revealed could no longer come to pass? Did you make peace with survival when God intended restoration?

This is your invitation to reconsider what you may have buried. To remember what God said, even if the road didn't go how you'd expected.

He hasn't changed his mind. His ways are higher. And his plans are still unfolding.

PRACTICAL WAYS TO LIVE WITH CERTAINTY

Certainty grows in practice. Not just in moments of revelation but in the quiet, repetitive decisions to keep aligning your life with what you Know.

It's like a muscle. You strengthen it by using it—consistently, intentionally, daily.

Here are a few ways to build a rhythm of certainty into your everyday life.

1. RETURN TO WHAT YOU KNOW

Certainty isn't about remembering everything all at once. It's about returning—again and again—to the truth that steadies you.

When your emotions rise, when life gets noisy, when doubt creeps in, come back to the last thing God made clear. Whether through journaling, quiet reflection, or simple stillness, build a space in your day to reset.

Ask yourself:

- What do I Know today—regardless of what's changed?
- What truth am I building from?

Certainty gets stronger every time you recenter your thoughts on the foundation of your Knowing.

2. LET YOUR WORDS STAY IN AGREEMENT

Back in chapter 10 we talked about how Knowing leads to saying and how what you speak shapes what you see.

That principle still holds. But here's where the practice gets real: Can you keep your words aligned with your Knowing even when the waiting gets long? Even when frustration creeps in?

Pay attention to your language. Not just what you say publicly but what you mutter under your breath. What you declare when you're tired. What you confess when no one is listening but heaven.

Ask yourself:

- Am I still speaking from what I Know?
- Or have I started adjusting my language to match my fear or fatigue?

You don't need to be loud, but you do need to be clear. Your words are construction tools. Make sure they're building the life you've been shown, not undoing it.

3. MAKE INTEGRITY-BASED DECISIONS

Certainty isn't just a feeling. It's a compass for your actions.

When you Know something deep in your spirit, your decisions should match that Knowing. This doesn't mean you'll always feel ready. It means you'll choose from alignment, not anxiety.

Integrity-based decisions are ones that move you forward with consistency, not convenience. So before you say yes, pause. Before you settle, ask again. Before you say, "It's good enough," hold it up to the light of your Knowing.

Ask yourself:

- Does this decision match my revelation?
- Will it move me toward the version of me I've seen, or away from it?

Certainty-based Knowing must eventually show up in values-based living.

4. PROTECT THE GATE OF YOUR CERTAINTY

Certainty is delicate in the wrong environment. You don't have to cut people off, but you do need to guard what you absorb.

Your certainty has gates. Eyes. Ears. Soul. Be wise about what you take in.

- What are you watching that feeds fear?
- What are you listening to that erodes your confidence?
- Who influences you, especially when you're vulnerable?

Certainty is not loud. It doesn't fight to be heard. So you have to make space for it on purpose. Surround yourself with soundness. Sound words. Sound voices. Sound relationships. You don't need everyone to agree with you, but you do need people who protect your alignment.

5. CREATE RITUALS OF ALIGNMENT

Certainty needs rhythm.

Not because God needs repetition but because we do. Our minds wander. Our hearts drift. Our focus gets fractured by life's demands.

So create practices that pull you back to center:

- Morning declarations over your Knowing
- Weekly reflection or stillness
- Gratitude lists
- Prayer walks
- "No phone" mornings
- Scriptural meditation

You don't need to do them all. Just find what recenters you and do it on purpose. Because the more your rhythm reflects your Knowing, the more your life will too.

CERTAINTY IN EVERY AREA OF LIFE

Knowing isn't meant to live in your journal. It's not just for quiet time or Sunday mornings. It's meant to move through you and shape how you show up everywhere.

When you're aligned with what God has revealed, it spills into every area of your life. Certainty in your relationships means you no longer settle for proximity without purpose. You don't cling to connections out of fear or habit. You pursue partnership that aligns with where you're going, not just where you've been.

It means you communicate with clarity. You set boundaries with peace. You give love from overflow, not from lack.

Certainty in your career or calling means you're not chasing everything. You're not reacting to what looks good or what everyone else is doing. You're building intentionally, in the direction of your assignment. You stop applying for roles that don't fit. You stop saying yes to what drains you. You start honoring your pace, protecting your energy, and stewarding the grace you've been given.

Certainty in your health means listening to your body without guilt, shame, or fear. You no longer treat wellness like punishment. You understand that if you're going to carry something heavy, you need strength. So you rest. You nourish. You move with intention, because your purpose matters.

Certainty in your finances means you sow with wisdom, spend with peace, and give without pressure. You don't chase money. You manage it. You make it submit to the life God showed you. And you trust that provision is part of the promise, not a prize for perfection.

Certainty in your parenting means you lead your children from Knowing, not from fear. You stop parenting from wounds you haven't healed. You listen differently. You correct from love, not ego. And you cover them in truth, because even your children are unfolding into purpose.

Certainty in your creativity means you no longer create to be seen. You create because there's something you Know that's too full to stay inside. You trust that the art, the words, the business, the vision will find its audience. Because you're not building for applause. You're building in obedience.

Certainty in your leadership means you're not leading to prove anything. You're not micromanaging out of insecurity. You're not performing for validation. You're moving with wisdom, delegating with trust, and leading people from a place of inner stability that inspires the same in others.

Certainty isn't a compartment. It's a current.

It runs through every conversation, every calendar decision, every yes, every no, every boundary, every opportunity.

And the more you build your life around what you Know, the more your life will reflect what God always knew about you.

CERTAINTY IS A PRACTICE, NOT A DESTINATION

You don't arrive at certainty. You practice it.

You don't "graduate" from Knowing. You grow deeper into it.

Certainty is not a place you land. It's a posture you return to over and over again. Knowing was never meant to be a moment, it was meant to be a movement within you. It's not just something you encounter. It's something you embody.

Even now there will be days when you forget. Moments that shake you. News that rattles your peace. Conversations that test your confidence. But that doesn't mean you've lost what you Know. It just means you're human. And as a human becoming, you will always need to realign.

This is why you don't wait to feel certain to live like it. You live like it because you Know. And when your Knowing wavers, you come back to what you've practiced. You remember what was revealed. You reset your rhythm. You rehearse your truth.

You start again.

That's how you build unshakable confidence. Not by knowing everything but by refusing to let go of what you do Know just because life gets loud. And when you build this way—with intention, with rhythm, with trust—you realize that certainty is not fragile. It's not shallow. It's not seasonal. It's anchored.

Because when you live aligned with your divine purpose, you're walking in the safest, strongest place you can be. That's what

Romans 8:28 is about: "And we know that in all things God works for the good of those who love him, who have been called according to his purpose" (NIV). We Know. We *Know.*

That means no matter what's happening in the world—in the economy, in the headlines, in the chaos—if you are walking in what God said, you are walking toward good.

You're not guessing. You're not gambling. You're not hoping the pieces might fit.

You're getting back to what has always been true: the good that God established from the beginning.

And not even the winds of this world can override what was written over you. You are called. You are kept. You are covered. And you are becoming—still.

So keep practicing. Keep walking. Keep Knowing.

The world may be uncertain, but you don't have to be.

FAREWELL

Well, beloved, our time together has come to an end. But I believe—deeply—that you'll never be the same. Not after the journey we've walked through in these pages. Not after what's been stirred, revealed, and remembered within you.

As you step forward into life with a new level of alignment, a deeper sense of Knowing, and a certainty you've never carried before, I want to speak these final words over you. A blessing. A covering. A reminder that what you Know will carry you through every season.

Receive this. Let it settle into your spirit.

May you walk forward, not with fear but with focus.

Not with striving but with stillness. Not with perfection but with certainty.

May the truth you carry be louder than the voices that doubt it.

May the word you've been given be stronger than the winds that try to move you.

May your Knowing rise in dark places, your voice speak what heaven has spoken, and your steps be steady, even when the path is still unfolding.

And when the world around you is uncertain, may the world within you remain unshaken.

You are not lost. You are not late. You are not alone.

You are walking in what God always knew about you. And every step you take from here is a step back to good.

Stay grounded. Stay faithful. And above all, keep practicing what you Know.

ACKNOWLEDGMENTS

FIRST AND FOREMOST I WANT TO EXPRESS MY DEEPEST gratitude to my Creator—the one who gave me this vision, this creativity, this voice, and this platform to birth a book I believe the world desperately needs in this hour.

God, I love you. Jesus, I praise you. I adore you.

To my incredible wife, Sarah—your support, your insight, your perspective, every conversation, every word of encouragement as I wrote took this book from amazing to exceptional. I love you deeply and immensely.

To Jan Miller—the one and only, unlike any other—thank you for being my literary agent, my advocate, and someone who continues to see me, believe in me, and create space for me to shine. You are a treasure. And thank you to the entire Dupree Miller team.

To my mother, Tommye Jean Williams—your thoughts, your wisdom, and your presence are invaluable to me. If you hadn't given your thumbs-up to each chapter as I texted them to you, I might not have moved forward. You are my North Star and have always been my anchor. I love you, and I pray this book makes you proud. Something tells me it does already.

To the amazing staff and teams I oversee, from Dallas to Los Angeles and beyond—thank you for your patience, your flexibility, and your faithfulness as I disappeared into the writing of this work. Your excellence is the infrastructure of my calling. I am honored to lead you.

To HarperCollins, HarperChristian, and Zondervan Books—thank you for your partnership over these past several years. You are the best in the business, and I'm grateful that, time and again, you've helped bring my vision to life with integrity and excellence.

To my children—you are my motivation. My inspiration. My everything. If you were the only ones to ever read this book, it would still have been worth writing. I cherish you. I believe in you. And I believe God has extraordinary plans for your lives.

And, finally, to every reader who invested in this book—thank you for investing in yourself. My prayer is that the return on that investment will exceed what you ever knew to ask for.

With love,
Touré

Balance

Positioning Yourself to Do All Things Well

Touré Roberts

Imagine learning to tap into the awareness, sensitivity, and highest thought patterns that enable the most successful outcomes in life, love, and business. What would your life look like if you were able to break the patterns of inconsistency that keep you from your absolute best? Could it be possible to identify and regularly access the highest version of yourself, leaving behind past hit-or-miss cycles and instead starting to win in every key area of your life?

These goals are not only possible, they are what you were made for!

In *Balance*, bestselling author Touré Roberts guides us on the eye-opening journey that unpacks the divine formula that makes this a reality.

This illuminating guide brings a unique and eye-opening perspective to the elusive concept of Balance. Transcending familiar theories of work-life balance, Roberts teaches that Balance is a state of existence, a becoming that, when realized, not only brings forth the highest version of an individual but also optimizes their life's output, productivity, relational value, and overall achievement.

As he unpacks Balance with stunning relatability, Roberts connects with readers on every level. His easy-to-grasp style of teaching and unabashed vulnerability illuminate and clarify how living in Balance is the longing in each human heart. Roberts shares life-changing personal stories and the principles they inspired while he was discovering Balance in his own life. As an author, speaker, entrepreneur, CEO, and lead pastor of two large congregations in the United States—as well as a devoted husband and dedicated father of six—Roberts knows that merely juggling responsibilities is not the answer.

Balance departs from traditional techniques of time management and better organization to get to the core issues at stake. Roberts reveals that the path to true balance prioritizes self and discovers the unique, deep internal needs of the individual first. "Identifying your deepest needs not only is life-transforming but brings forth your greatest self, pouring an overflow of your best and highest abilities into the lives of everyone around you," Roberts explains. "Balance is not about learning to effectively give pieces of yourself to important parts of your life. Balance is about knowing and becoming your entire self—and then giving from your wholeness to everyone and everything within the context of your life."

Key chapters include "The Power of No," which unpacks why *no* is the most powerful word in your vocabulary; "There's No Team in I," a liberating and paradigm-shifting exploration of the difference between being selfish and the transformational quality of a term Roberts coins as being "self-ful"; "The Five Signs of Imbalance," which will help you quickly identify the imbalances in your life and effectively respond before crisis hits; and "Balance After the Blow," a step-by-step guide to get you back on your feet after experiencing an unexpected setback. You'll walk away from each illuminating chapter with powerful principles, tools, and prompts for self-evaluation.

A personal navigation guide like no other, *Balance* charts your course to productivity, peace, positivity, purpose, and unlimited possibilities.

Wholeness

Winning in Life from the Inside Out

Touré Roberts

Wholeness is about removing invisible boundaries from our lives that keep us from realizing our highest potential. In order to live an outer life without limits, we have to uncover and address the inner limitations that hide in our blind spots.

This life-changing book explains that regardless of where you are in life, Wholeness will take you higher. Wholeness will elevate your sense of fulfillment in life, produce healthier, more rewarding relationships, and position you for optimum success in every endeavor.

International thought leader and pastor Touré Roberts explains we can't always choose the experiences that keep us from being whole, but we can take control of our lives today and bring healing to any broken area. Key chapters include an in-depth relationship guide titled "Two Halves Don't Make a Whole." "The Cracked Mirror" shows how unprocessed experiences can negatively shape our view of self, others, and the world around us. "Ghosts of the Past" gives powerful, practical tools for avoiding the traps of the past and ensuring that we enter the amazing future that God has planned for us.

Wholeness is filled with wisdom garnered from Touré's own life—raised by a single mom, narrowly escaping the traps of inner-city life, and finding success in corporate America. His insight is further broadened by his role as founder of one of the most influential churches in the nation, with more than fourteen years pastoring thousands of millennials, couples, families, and a diverse group of individuals. *Wholeness* will take you on a transformational journey that won't leave you the same.

Concluding with a "Wholeness Test," *Wholeness* will help you track and maintain your progress while walking out your journey to your full potential.

Available in stores and online!

ZONDERVAN®